Rethink Consumption

Oliver Hoffmann

Rethink Consumption

How to take back control of your consumer behavior

Oliver Hoffmann 
London, UK

ISBN 978-3-662-72945-8   ISBN 978-3-662-72946-5   (eBook)
https://doi.org/10.1007/978-3-662-72946-5

Conflict of Interest The author has no conflicts of interest relevant to the content of this manuscript.

Five Facts About Addiction to Consumption

1. **Excessive Consumption and Debt**
   According to the Federal Centre for Health Education (BZgA) and the Institute for Financial Services (iff), there are alarming figures regarding over-indebtedness in Germany. In 2023, approximately 18.4% of the German population were over-indebted due to addictive behaviors, including compulsive buying. Those most affected are people living alone, who on average are in debt by €30,000.[1]

2. **Rising Compulsive Buying Worldwide**
   Worldwide, between 5% and 8% of people suffer from compulsive buying or display problematic purchasing behavior; the number of unreported cases may be even higher, as the issue is still either normalized or associated with strong feelings of shame and guilt. This addiction particularly affects younger people and women, who are especially strongly influenced by digital media.[2]

3. **Luxury Goods and Status Consumption**
   The market for luxury goods reached a record value of 1.4 trillion US dollars in 2023. The majority of this growth is driven by consumers who purchase luxury goods not out of practical need, but to demonstrate their social status. This "conspicuous consumption" has increased significantly over the past decades.[3]

---

[1] IFF Over-Indebtedness Report 2023.

[2] MHH (2021): Compulsive Buying: On the Way to Becoming a Recognized Disorder.

[3] BZgA. (2023): Compulsive Buying and Debt: When Consumption Becomes an Illness.

4. **Psychological Strain from Compulsive Consumption**

   According to a study by the American Psychological Association (APA), over 80% of people with compulsive buying disorder also suffer from depression, anxiety disorders, or other mental illnesses. Compulsive consumption is often used as a coping strategy for negative emotions, which, however, leads to a vicious cycle.[4]

5. **The Power of Online Consumption**

   In 2023, 82% of the German population aged between 16 and 74 reported having shopped online. "Buy now, pay later" models encourage uncontrolled consumption and debt, as they blur the line between the purchase decision and the actual payment.[5]

---

[4] American Psychological Association (APA) (2021): The impact of compulsive buying on mental health.

[5] AOK (2023): Compulsive Buying and Online Shopping.

Contents

1

Introduction

Abstract The introduction of the book makes it clear that consumption is more than just a means of satisfying needs—it is an integral part of our self-concept, our social relationships, and our cultural identity. In a world where advertising and social media dominate our everyday consumption, reflecting on consumption habits becomes all the more important. Addiction to consumption is examined as a serious issue that has not only individual but also societal causes. In this context, consumption is understood as culturally normalized behavior that shapes identity, status, and group affiliation. The introduction makes it clear that consumption habits are not solely the result of individual choices, but are also promoted by social and economic structures. The guide aims to help readers think more critically about their own consumption behavior and to develop practical strategies for change.

Consumption permeates all areas of our lives. It shapes not only our individual behavior, but also our social relationships, cultural norms, and societal structures. What we buy, how we consume, and the value we assign to things are central questions that encompass not only economic but also psychological dimensions. In an era where advertising, social media, and economic incentives relentlessly urge us to own more and consume more, reflecting on our consumption behavior is more relevant than ever.

This book explores the question of why consumption is far more for many people than the mere acquisition of goods to satisfy needs. It analyzes the psychological mechanisms underlying our consumption behavior

O. Hoffmann, *Rethink Consumption*, https://doi.org/10.1007/978-3-662-72946-5_1

and shows how deeply these are intertwined with fundamental human needs such as belonging, recognition, and identity. At the same time, it highlights how external factors such as marketing strategies, cultural narratives, and technological developments are deliberately designed to influence our decisions and shape our consumption patterns.

A particular focus is placed on the social phenomenon of compulsive buying disorder—a state in which the urge to consume is no longer rational or controlled, but driven by internal compulsions and emotional needs. Compulsive buying is considered here not only as an individual problem, but as a symptom of a society that, in many ways, is oriented toward abundance and constant availability. It becomes clear that the problem does not lie solely in individual behavior, but in a system that elevates consumption to the central maxim.

But this book does not stop at analysis. It offers concrete approaches to critically question your own consumption, change habits, and lead a more conscious life. Readers are invited to redefine their relationship to possessions and consumption. The aim is not to demonize consumption per se, but to bring it into a balance that connects personal satisfaction with social responsibility.

With a combination of scientific insights, practical exercises, and reflective questions, this book is both a theoretical guide and a practical tool. It is aimed at anyone who feels overwhelmed by their consumption behavior, those who want to make more conscious decisions, and those seeking a more sustainable lifestyle. It is a call to regain control over your own decisions and to develop a new, self-determined perspective on consumption and possessions. For the first step toward change begins with the realization that we are more than what we own.

1.1   Why this Book?

> **Example**
>
> In this section, you will learn why it is important to address the issue of compulsive buying and which fundamental questions this book seeks to answer.

Compulsive buying is not a topic limited to individuals. It is a mirror of our times, both a symptom and a driving force of our modern society. In a world where consumption has become the defining factor for identity, status, and even personal happiness, it seems paradoxical to talk about compulsive buying—because the act of consuming is highly valued socially, even almost required. Yet it is precisely in this supposed normality that the danger lies: compulsive buying is rarely recognized as a problem because it is deeply embedded in the structures that define our lives. So why this book? Because it is time to lift the veil and confront the psychological, social, and economic mechanisms that not only enable this addiction but actively drive it forward.

The modern world confronts us with a constant flood of products, advertising messages, and social media that incessantly encourage us to buy more, own more, and seek our happiness in the endless aisles of the consumer market. Consumption is no longer just an act of meeting needs, but has become a central means of self-presentation and social distinction. Yet this process is by no means harmless. Studies show that up to eight percent of people exhibit problematic buying behavior, which in severe cases leads to over-indebtedness, social isolation, and mental illness (Köhler, 2020). Compulsive buying is not only an individual crisis but also a societal one, threatening our economic and ecological balance.

Imagine you go into a department store and buy a new jacket you don't need, but which gives you, for a brief moment, the feeling of being someone else—more successful, more attractive, or simply happier. This high quickly fades, but the urge remains. Again and again, people seek this short-term satisfaction, a quick rush of happiness that buying promises but rarely delivers. The mechanism behind this is alarmingly effective: the reward system in our brain responds to the act of buying by releasing dopamine, a neurotransmitter that conveys happiness and satisfaction (Schmidt, 2019). But this effect is fleeting, and soon a craving for more sets in—a vicious cycle that intensifies in a spiral.

A practical example illustrates how profound these mechanisms are. A young woman, let's call her Anna, reports her experience with online shopping. At first, she only occasionally bought clothes or accessories, but over time she developed a real addiction. She began spending hours every day in online shops, often late into the night. Her credit card bills grew ever higher, and she started hiding her purchases from friends and family. "It was as if I was losing control over my life," Anna describes. Her case is not an isolated one, but a typical example of the dynamics of compulsive buying: a short-lived high, followed by guilt and despair.

> **Important**
>
> Compulsive buying is not simply an individual failure, but an expression of social pressures and economic structures. Recognizing this is the first step toward change.

This book is not intended to be just another work pointing out the dark sides of consumerism, but rather a tool to initiate sustainable change. Compulsive buying is not an isolated issue, but a phenomenon deeply rooted in our psyche, our social structures, and the mechanisms of the modern economy. It does not arise in a vacuum, but is intensified by targeted manipulation: by advertising that creates needs we never had, by social media that suggests an unattainable ideal of wealth and happiness, and by a culture that defines status and identity through possessions.

But compulsive buying is more than just accumulating things. It is an expression of emptiness, insecurity, and the search for meaning. People do not just buy products—they buy promises: the promise of belonging, recognition, control, or even love. This book addresses precisely this point and invites you to understand the psychology behind these dynamics. It shows why buying things makes us happy in the short term, but often leaves us feeling emptier in the long run.

Over the course of the chapters, you will delve deeply into the structures of consumerism. You will understand how our brains respond to advertising messages, why social comparisons fuel the urge for more, and how consumerism is used as a form of distraction from emotional challenges. At the same time, practical exercises and strategies will be presented to help you question and reshape your own consumption patterns.

Mindfulness plays a central role in this. By becoming more aware of your emotions, impulses, and decision-making processes, you can learn to regain control over your actions. This book shows how you can develop consumer competence: the ability to consciously decide what you really need and to detach yourself from what only promises short-term satisfaction. This includes techniques for reflection, methods for reducing external influences, and concrete steps to sustainably change consumption behavior.

The way out of the consumption trap is not easy, but it is possible. It begins with the realization that true value does not lie in things, but in experiences, relationships, and personal growth. This book gives you tools to put this insight into practice and fundamentally rethink your relationship to possessions and consumption. It becomes clear that it is not just about personal gain. By rethinking your consumption, you also contribute to a fairer and more sustainable world.

By the end of this book, you will not only understand why you consume, but also how you can gain the freedom to consume less—and live more.

Summary

This section has outlined why compulsive buying is a central issue of our time and why it is necessary to address its causes and consequences. With this book, I aim to offer a new perspective and practical ways to overcome it.

1.2   Is Consumption Really an Addiction?

Example

In this section, you will learn what distinguishes compulsive buying from other forms of addiction and why it is often trivialized, even though it has profound effects on individual and societal life.

A deeper understanding of compulsive buying requires a look at the underlying psychological mechanisms and social dynamics that foster this behavior. Compulsive buying is not an isolated phenomenon, but is closely linked to emotional, cognitive, and social factors. Many affected individuals report that the act of buying is a means of coping with stress, loneliness, or inner emptiness. In modern consumer societies, the act of buying has developed into far more than a simple means of satisfying needs. Instead, it often fulfills a symbolic function deeply rooted in our psychological mechanisms. We do not just buy to own or use something, but because we associate an emotional and cognitive projection with the acquired object. This projection may include the promise of happiness, social recognition, or personal improvement. Yet this notion often remains an illusion.

In moments of emotional strain or inner emptiness, the act of buying serves as a short-term strategy to compensate for negative feelings. Stress, loneliness, frustration, or self-doubt can be temporarily alleviated by the apparent comfort of a new object. This process is often reinforced by advertising messages that link products with ideals such as success, beauty, or joy of life. In this context, a particular item becomes a symbol for what one supposedly wants to achieve in life.

The problem, however, lies in the fleeting nature of this relief. The joy of acquisition is often short-lived and is quickly replaced by feelings such as guilt, shame, or frustration. These negative emotions arise from the discrepancy between the high expectations attached to the purchase and the reality that the object could not fulfill those expectations. This emotional imbalance can, in turn, lead to another purchase seeming like the solution, thus creating a vicious cycle.

This cycle of addictive behavior is reinforced by the way our brain responds to consumption. Neuroscientific studies show that the act of buying activates the reward system, particularly the release of dopamine, a neurotransmitter associated with pleasure and motivation. But as soon as the purchase is completed and the initial dopamine rush subsides, an emotional downturn occurs, which can trigger the need for a new source of reward. In this way, addictive consumption behavior becomes entrenched.

The psychological mechanisms that maintain compulsive buying are similar to those described in classical addiction research. The brain learns to associate the act of buying with a feeling of reward, and this conditioned stimulus increasingly becomes the driving force behind the behavior. At the same time, the ability for self-control decreases, as the neurobiological processes responsible for impulse control and decision-making are impaired by repeated addictive behavior. This loss of control is a central indicator that compulsive buying goes far beyond a simple weakness or lack of discipline.

What makes compulsive buying unique, however, is its cultural context. In a world shaped by advertising, social media, and an almost unlimited supply of goods, consumption is portrayed as an everyday norm. Advertising suggests that happiness, satisfaction, and social status can be achieved through the possession of certain products. This social pressure reinforces the behaviors of people already prone to addictive patterns and makes it harder for them to break free from these influences. Another factor that intensifies compulsive buying is the increasing digitization of consumption. Online shopping platforms and personalized algorithms create an environment designed to promote impulse purchases. Through targeted recommendations and easy payment methods, the buying process is made so seamless that it hardly requires conscious decisions. For people already inclined toward compulsive buying, this digital environment offers almost perfect conditions to intensify their behavior. The societal consequences of compulsive buying are as serious as the individual ones. In addition to the financial burden, which often leads to debt, excessive consumption also causes ecological problems. The relentless drive for new products significantly contributes to the overuse of natural resources and environmental pollution. Compulsive buying is therefore not only an individual but also a systemic problem that requires a holistic approach and solution.

A critical examination of compulsive buying requires us to question both the psychological foundations and the social structures that promote this behavior. The first step is to recognize compulsive buying as a serious issue that cannot be solved by simple appeals to self-control. Rather, an approach is needed that considers both the individual psyche and the societal framework. Only through a combination of psychological support, education, and political action can we break the cycle of compulsive buying and pave the way to a more conscious, sustainable lifestyle.

A particularly clear example of the normalization of compulsive buying can be found in the area of online shopping. Platforms like Amazon or Zalando make it easier than ever to purchase goods. Constant availability, personalized recommendations, and "buy now, pay later" models encourage impulsive buying and exacerbate dependency. A young man, let's call him Tobias, described his experience with such platforms: "I started ordering something almost every day. It was so easy, and it felt like a little reward every time. But at the end of the month, I was always shocked at how much money I had spent." Tobias's story is not unique. It illustrates how the combination of technological availability and psychological mechanisms can lead to a vicious cycle that is hard to break.

> **Example**
>
> Note: Compulsive buying is often trivialized because it is embedded in the context of an accepted and even encouraged behavior. This makes it all the more important to raise awareness of its risks.

Another crucial factor contributing to the trivialization of compulsive buying is its seemingly harmless nature. Unlike alcohol or drug addiction, the direct physical harm is often not obvious. Yet the long-term consequences can be just as devastating: over-indebtedness, social isolation, and mental illnesses such as depression and anxiety disorders are just some of the risks. Moreover, compulsive buying has profound effects on the environment, as it leads to an ever-escalating demand for resources and the production of waste. The ecological dimension of compulsive buying is often ignored, as the focus is on individual consequences.

So why is compulsive buying so often trivialized? One reason lies in the deep entrenchment of consumerism in our society. Advertising and social media propagate an image in which consumption is not only normal but desirable. The possession of goods is equated with success, happiness, and social recognition. This cultural glorification of consumption makes it difficult to draw the line between healthy buying behavior and addictive consumption. In addition, many affected individuals do not recognize their addiction as such, since they operate in a social environment that promotes and rewards excessive buying.

Reference to Exercise 1

In Sect. 9.3.1 "Strengthening Mindfulness in Buying Behavior," you will find a first practical exercise to help you become more aware of and reflect on your buying impulses. This exercise supports you in identifying emotional triggers for impulsive buying and developing alternative strategies to establish a healthier consumption pattern in the long term.

To better understand the dynamics of compulsive buying, it helps to look at its psychological mechanisms. A central aspect is the concept of hedonic adaptation, which describes how quickly people get used to new possessions and thus develop the desire for even more goods (Frederick & Loewenstein, 1999). This mechanism drives the constant cycle of buying and reinforces dependency. Added to this is the role of social comparison: in a world where social media provides constant insight into the lives of others, there is enormous pressure to keep up with consumer-oriented lifestyles. This pressure intensifies compulsive buying and leads to an ever-increasing focus on material values (Müller, 2021).

Summary

- Compulsive buying differs from other forms of addiction due to its close cultural and societal context, in which consumption is not only tolerated but actively promoted, which encourages the trivialization of this issue.
- The psychological mechanisms behind compulsive buying, such as the association of buying actions with short-term reward and the role of hedonic adaptation, lead to a vicious cycle of consumption and emotional setbacks.
- Compulsive buying has profound individual, social, and ecological effects, ranging from financial burdens and mental illnesses to overuse of resources and environmental destruction.

Compulsive buying is a complex and often underestimated form of dependency that is deeply embedded in our culture. Its trivialization lies in its social acceptance and the difficulty of recognizing its negative effects. This section has shown why it is necessary to take compulsive buying seriously and to question its mechanisms.

1.3 What can you Expect from this Guide?

> **Example**
>
> In this section, you will learn how this book is structured, what practical help it offers, and how you can use it to regain control over your consumption behavior.

Dealing with compulsive and luxury consumption is a complex process that requires both knowledge and reflection, as well as concrete steps for action. However, this book is not a theoretical work that focuses solely on analysis, but primarily a practical, clearly written guide designed to help you sustainably change your consumption behavior. At its core is the question: How can we develop a conscious and healthy approach to our resources in a society that glorifies consumption? This book gives you the tools to answer this question for yourself.

First, you will develop a comprehensive understanding of the mechanisms behind compulsive and luxury consumption. For only those who recognize the causes and dynamics of these behaviors can find ways to break free from them. The book begins with a clear definition and distinction between compulsive and luxury consumption. It examines how emotional, social, and cultural factors influence our purchasing decisions and the role psychological mechanisms play. It also addresses the subtle manipulations that are intensified by advertising and social media.

In this context, Chap. 2 (Understanding Compulsive and Luxury Consumption) as well as Chap. 4 (The Causes of Addiction), Chap. 5 (The Way Out of the Consumption Trap), and Chap. 7 (Long-Term Change) are the core chapters that build on each other and convey the most essential content, while the other chapters address supplementary aspects.

Another integral part of this book is practical exercises and instructions to help you reflect on your own consumption behavior. You will receive checklists (Sect. 9.2) that show you whether you are at risk of developing compulsive buying and what first steps you can take to regain control. These tools are designed to be easily integrated into everyday life and provide you with concrete guidance.

Particularly important is the development of strategies to reduce impulsive buying behavior. Here you will learn how mindfulness and conscious decision-making can help you distinguish between real needs and manipulative consumption incentives. Financial self-control is another key focus: this book shows you how to regain an overview of your finances and develop a sustainable budget that reflects your values and goals.

Practical Tip

The exercises in this book should not be seen as one-off tasks. Repetition and continuity are crucial for achieving lasting change. Take your time and proceed step by step. Also read Sect. 1.4.

Special attention is also given to alternative lifestyles. Minimalism and sustainable consumption are introduced as concepts that not only reduce material possessions but can also lead to greater quality of life and satisfaction. You will discover how a conscious approach to consumption can help you define your values more clearly and lead a more authentic life.

At the end of this book, the question is how you can anchor long-term changes in your consumption behavior. Relapses are part of any change, and this book shows you how to deal with them and learn from them. The goal is not just to achieve short-term success, but to develop a new attitude toward consumption that gives you long-term freedom and self-determination.

Summary

This book is your companion on the path to a more conscious and self-determined life. It provides you with the knowledge, tools, and inspiration you need to question and sustainably change your consumption habits.

1.4   Notes on the Practical Exercises

The practical exercises included in the book are designed to help you develop a deeper understanding of your personal consumption patterns and establish alternative strategies to help you approach your buying behavior more consciously. Each exercise is designed to be applicable regardless of your current life situation and can be carried out both in everyday life and during quiet periods of reflection.

1. **Individuality of the exercises:**
   The exercises are designed to be flexible and can be adapted to your individual needs. There is no "right" or "wrong" way to do them. What matters is that you take your time, are honest with yourself, and view your experiences without self-judgment.

2. **Regular application:**
   To achieve long-term change, it makes sense to repeat the exercises regularly. Consumption patterns and deeply rooted habits take time to change. Continuity helps you solidify new ways of thinking and behaving.

3. **Journaling and reflection:**
   It can be helpful to keep a journal or notebook in which you record your thoughts, feelings, and insights during the exercises. This allows you to document progress and more easily recognize recurring patterns.

4. **Openness and curiosity:**
   Approach the exercises with an open attitude. The goal is not to judge yourself, but to learn more about your relationship to consumption. See the exercises as an opportunity to get to know yourself better and gain new perspectives.

5. **Integration into everyday life:**
   Many exercises can be integrated into your daily life without much time investment. Some are designed to be carried out spontaneously, for example during shopping or while scrolling through online shops. This everyday perspective enables you to make conscious decisions directly in the situation.

6. **Support and exchange:**
   If you feel challenged, do not hesitate to exchange ideas with others or, if necessary, consider professional support. Dialogue with friends, family, or a professional can help broaden your perspectives and provide additional suggestions.

7. **Patience with yourself:**
   Changes in consumption behavior require time and patience. It is normal to experience setbacks or occasionally feel discouraged. Use such moments to pause and remind yourself that every conscious reflection is a step in the right direction.

The exercises are intended not only to provide you with practical tools, but also to help you develop a deeper understanding of the psychological and emotional mechanisms behind your consumption behavior. They are an essential part of the path to a more conscious and sustainable approach to consumption.

References

Frederick, S., & Loewenstein, G. (1999): *Hedonic adaptation. Well-being: The foundations of hedonic psychology*. Russell Sage Foundation.

Köhler, M. (2020). *Kaufsucht und Gesellschaft: Eine psychologische Analyse*. Springer.

Müller, S. (2021). *Die Psychologie des Kaufens: Warum wir Dinge wollen, die wir nicht brauchen*. Hanser.

Schmidt, L. (2019). *Neuropsychologie des Konsums: Wie unser Gehirn den Markt formt*. Beltz.

2

Understanding Consumption and Luxury Addiction

Abstract This chapter is dedicated to a detailed analysis of consumer and luxury addiction. A distinction is made between compulsive consumption as an individual coping strategy and luxury consumption as a means of social distinction. While consumer addiction is often characterized by impulsive purchasing decisions and emotional regulation, luxury consumption in many cases serves external status demonstration and symbolic self-presentation. Psychological mechanisms such as dopamine release during the act of purchasing or social comparison dynamics are explained. It is also shown how advertising and social media systematically manipulate consumer behavior to intensify the pursuit of new goods and a prestigious lifestyle. The effects of these mechanisms range from individual financial strain to ecological consequences.

Consumption is a central component of modern life that goes far beyond the mere satisfaction of material needs. It serves as a means of expressing identity, social belonging, and status, and reflects the values and norms of our society. But what happens when consumption departs from its original function and becomes an addiction? This chapter is dedicated to a comprehensive analysis of consumption and luxury addiction, their causes, and their effects on the individual and society.

The Psychological Dimension of Consumption Addiction
Consumer behavior is deeply rooted in our emotional and psychological mechanisms. People do not buy solely to satisfy a need, but also to

O. Hoffmann, *Rethink Consumption*, https://doi.org/10.1007/978-3-662-72946-5_2

compensate for emotional deficits. Feelings such as stress, insecurity, loneliness, or inner emptiness can be temporarily alleviated by the act of purchasing. This dynamic is based on the activation of the brain's reward system: buying an object triggers the release of dopamine, which provides a short-term feeling of joy or relief. However, this satisfaction is usually only short-lived. As soon as dopamine levels drop again, the original negative feelings return, often accompanied by guilt or shame over the expenditures made. This cycle leads to an increased urge to buy and fosters the development of addictive behavior.

Luxury Addiction: The Drive for Prestige and Recognition

Luxury addiction is a specific form of consumption addiction that is particularly closely linked to the need for social status and recognition. Luxury goods symbolize success, power, and exclusivity, thus fulfilling not only material but above all symbolic functions. The acquisition of luxury items is often used as a means to bridge social distance, signal belonging, or boost one's self-esteem. In this context, the staging of consumption—such as on social media—is playing an increasingly important role. Studies show that the perception of luxury is often more important than the actual utility of the products. This dynamic leads many people to exceed their financial limits in order to meet the expectations of their social environment.

The Role of Advertising and Social Media

The advertising industry and social media significantly reinforce the mechanisms of consumption and luxury addiction. Advertising is designed to create needs that did not previously exist and to link products with emotional promises. Slogans such as "Because you're worth it" or "The best for you" appeal to the need for self-worth and individuality. At the same time, social media creates a stage on which consumption is used to showcase one's lifestyle. Influencers and advertising campaigns present consumption as the key to a happy, successful life, increasing the pressure to conform to this ideal.

The Societal Impact of Consumption and Luxury Addiction

The normalization of excessive consumption has far-reaching consequences for society. On the one hand, it leads to increased social inequality, as not everyone can afford the desired lifestyle. On the other hand, it has significant ecological consequences, as the constant demand for new products overuses resources and contributes to environmental destruction. The focus on material possessions also diverts attention from immaterial values such as relationships, creativity, or personal development.

Reflection and Change of Perspective

A deeper understanding of the dynamics behind consumption and luxury addiction is the first step toward breaking free from these dependencies. It requires critically questioning one's own consumption behavior and becoming aware of the emotional and social needs underlying this behavior. This chapter invites you to reflect on the role of consumption in your own life and to find alternative ways to experience belonging, self-worth, and fulfillment—beyond material possessions.

The goal is not to avoid consumption entirely, but to develop a more conscious, reflective approach that aligns with one's own values and needs. By understanding the mechanisms of consumption and luxury addiction, we can regain control over our behavior and promote a more sustainable lifestyle.

2.1   What Is Consumption Addiction— and How Does It Differ from Luxury Addiction?

> **Example**
>
> In this section, you will learn about the fundamental differences between consumption addiction and luxury addiction and discover how both phenomena affect individuals and society.

Consumption addiction and luxury addiction are two phenomena that at first glance display similar patterns, but differ significantly in their underlying motivations and effects. Both forms of behavior are based on excessive and often compulsive engagement with the consumption of goods, serving as means of emotional regulation or social self-presentation. Their differences are not only analytically significant, but also crucial for understanding the psychological mechanisms driving these behaviors, as well as for approaches to prevention and therapy.

Consumption addiction is characterized by a **fixation on the act of buying itself.** It manifests in impulsive, uncontrolled purchases that often do not correspond to an actual need for the acquired products. Here, the focus is less on the quality or social status of the goods and more on the quick and immediate gratification promised by the act of buying. Studies show that the brain's reward system is activated in consumers as soon as a purchase is made. This dopamine release creates a short-term feeling of happiness and relief, but it quickly fades, leading to the urge for further purchases (Schmidt, 2019). Consumption addiction is therefore often closely linked to emotional deficits, such as low self-esteem, stress, or a deeply felt inner emptiness. Those affected use the act of buying as a coping strategy, which, however, does not provide a sustainable solution and often leads to financial problems and social isolation.

Luxury addiction, on the other hand, is more **symbolic and strategic** in nature. The focus here is not on the purchasing process itself, but on the meaning and external impact of the acquired goods. People with a tendency toward luxury addiction invest in high-priced, exclusive, or hard-to-obtain products that serve less of a functional purpose and more as status symbols. These products are intended to signal power, success, or belonging and are often deliberately presented in social contexts to strengthen or define one's position (Belk, 1988). Unlike consumption addiction, where impulsivity plays a central role, luxury purchases are often planned and specifically aimed at gaining social recognition. Social pressure and the increasing prevalence of idealized lifestyles on social media reinforce this dynamic. Platforms such as Instagram or TikTok contribute to luxury addiction being perceived as an acceptable or even admirable behavior, making self-recognition and treatment more difficult.

Despite their differences, there are **overlaps** between the two phenomena, particularly regarding their underlying function. Both behaviors aim to compensate for emotional or social deficits. However, they differ in the way these needs are expressed and satisfied. While consumption addiction is often seen as an individual coping strategy, luxury addiction is more socially embedded and shaped by social norms and expectations. These differences have important implications for prevention and intervention. Approaches that focus on impulse control and the promotion of emotional resilience in consumption addiction must be supplemented in luxury addiction by measures that question social pressure and the cultural idealization of luxury goods.

The distinction between consumption addiction and luxury addiction is therefore by no means trivial. It not only reflects different psychological mechanisms, but also points to the complex social and cultural dynamics that shape our consumption behavior. A deep understanding of these differences makes it possible to develop individually tailored strategies that can be applied both at the level of affected individuals and at the societal level. Reflection on these phenomena should therefore not only aim to change individual behavior, but also to critically question the structural and normative frameworks that promote consumption and luxury.

Consumption addiction is often the result of a deeply rooted need for short-term gratification. Studies show that many affected individuals experience momentary relief from stress, anxiety, or inner emptiness through the act of buying (Müller, 2021). The brain's reward system is activated, creating a sense of control and satisfaction that is, however, only short-lived. Consumption addiction can manifest in a variety of behaviors, from impulsive buying to outright shopping sprees, which often end in financial problems and social isolation. Its trivialization in society makes it harder for those affected to recognize the problem and seek help.

Luxury addiction is a phenomenon deeply rooted in social structures and shaped by social and cultural values. In contrast to consumption addiction, where the act of buying is central, luxury addiction focuses on the symbolic meaning of the acquired goods. Luxury goods are primarily perceived as status symbols intended to convey power, success, and social belonging. Here, the value of a product is defined not only by its functionality, but above all by its exclusivity and the symbolic power associated with it. Luxury addiction is often closely linked to social pressure and social comparison, which are reinforced by social media and advertising (Frederick & Loewenstein, 1999). It can lead those affected into a spiral of financial overextension and social competition.

A striking example is the purchase of an expensive sports car. For many buyers, this car is much more than a means of transportation—it becomes an expression of success and individuality. The same applies to designer handbags, which are purchased less for their practical function and more as a visible sign of style and wealth. This type of consumption is closely linked to social perception: owning such goods not only signals one's social status but also fulfills the need for recognition and admiration.

Luxury addiction is further reinforced by social pressure and social comparison. In a world increasingly shaped by social media, there is a constant competition for the best, most successful, or most glamorous life. Platforms such as Instagram or TikTok provide a stage on which luxury goods are deliberately showcased to gain attention and recognition. Studies show that these social comparisons can significantly increase the desire for prestigious consumer goods (Belk, 2013). Constantly scrolling through images of trips to five-star resorts, expensive jewelry, or luxurious dinner parties creates in many the feeling of having to keep up—a dynamic that greatly increases the pressure to acquire such goods. Another characteristic of luxury addiction is its ability to create financial and social risks. The urge to keep up or improve one's position often leads to a spiral of financial overextension. Many people invest in expensive goods that exceed their financial means and thus fall into debt. At the same time, such purchases intensify social competition, as they not only operate at the individual level but also shape societal expectations and norms. Those who refuse to acquire luxury risk being perceived as less successful or ambitious, which further increases social pressure. The symbolic meaning of luxury goods is also culturally shaped. In some societies, they are considered indispensable indicators of success and status, while in others, modesty and restraint are valued more highly. In Western societies, the possession of luxury goods is often associated with the pursuit of individuality and self-actualization. These narratives are further reinforced by advertising and marketing strategies that specifically target the emotional and social significance of luxury goods. A well-known campaign for luxury watches, for example, advertises with the slogan: "It's not the time you own—it's the story you tell." Such messages make it clear that buying luxury is not just about the product, but about presenting an identity. Luxury addiction is not only an individual phenomenon, but also has profound societal effects. It promotes a materialistic worldview in which a person's value is increasingly measured by their possessions. This can exacerbate social inequalities, as access to luxury goods remains unattainable for many people. At the same time, the production and consumption of such goods contribute significantly to environmental burdens, as their manufacture is often resource-intensive and entails high environmental costs.

> **Reference to Exercise 2**
>
> To develop a deeper awareness of your personal consumption patterns and their underlying triggers, Exercise 2: "Analysis of Your Own Consumption Behavior" is recommended. This practical exercise, which can be found in Sect. 9.3.2, supports you in questioning impulsive and strategic purchasing decisions, recognizing emotional and social backgrounds, and developing alternative strategies for more conscious consumption. It offers you a structured way to reflect on your relationship to consumption and possessions, to classify dependencies, and to take initial steps toward a more sustainable and satisfying lifestyle.

A practical example illustrates the differences: A person suffering from consumption addiction might impulsively and thoughtlessly buy several items of clothing that they neither need nor can afford. A person with luxury addiction, on the other hand, would strategically and deliberately invest in an expensive watch to convey a particular image of success and exclusivity. While both behaviors are problematic, they differ in their underlying motivations and social dynamics.

Important

Consumption addiction and luxury addiction should not be viewed in isolation. The two phenomena often overlap, and those affected may exhibit characteristics of both dependencies. This makes differentiated analysis and an individual approach all the more important.

The social effects of both phenomena are profound. Consumption addiction contributes to the waste of resources, overproduction, and ultimately to environmental pollution. It reflects a culture of abundance that is oriented toward short-term gratification rather than long-term sustainability. Luxury addiction, on the other hand, intensifies social inequalities and promotes a materialistic worldview that measures a person's value by their possessions. Both addictions contribute to individuals feeling trapped in a cycle of unfulfilled needs and ever-new purchases, which has not only personal but also societal consequences.

In Summary

Consumption addiction and luxury addiction are distinct but interconnected phenomena, each bringing specific challenges and risks.

Consumption addiction is characterized by a fixation on the act of buying itself, which occurs impulsively and uncontrollably, without an actual need for the acquired products. The purchase serves the short-term satisfaction of emotional needs and is often used as a coping strategy for stress, low self-esteem, or inner emptiness. This process is reinforced by the release of dopamine in the brain, which provides a brief feeling of happiness and relief, but quickly fades and reignites the cycle of addictive behavior. In the long term, consumption addiction often leads to financial problems and social isolation.

Luxury addiction, on the other hand, focuses less on the purchasing process itself and more on the symbolic meaning of the acquired goods. High-priced products primarily serve as status symbols to signal power, success, or belonging. Luxury purchases are usually strategically planned and aimed at social recognition. Social media reinforce this dynamic by propagating idealized lifestyles that normalize or make luxury consumption appear admirable.

Although consumption addiction and luxury addiction differ in their expression and motivation, they share the function of compensating for emotional or social deficits. While consumption addiction is primarily individual and impulsive, luxury addiction is more strongly shaped by societal norms and expectations. Prevention and intervention approaches must take these differences into account: consumption addiction requires measures to strengthen emotional resilience and impulse control, while in luxury addiction, social pressure and the cultural idealization of luxury goods should be questioned. This section has illuminated the underlying mechanisms and social effects and shown why it is important to consider both forms of dependency in a differentiated manner.

2.2   The Psychology Behind Shopping Addiction: Emotions, Status, and Need Fulfillment

Example

In this section, you will learn how emotional and cognitive processes influence our consumer behavior and why we often buy more than we actually need.

Shopping addiction is a multifactorial phenomenon that is deeply rooted in the emotional and cognitive processes of humans. The act of purchasing is often perceived as an act of self-empowerment or reward, but in reality, it frequently serves to fulfill emotional needs that go far beyond material utility. Emotions such as joy, comfort, stress relief, or the need for belonging play a central role. The human brain responds to the act of buying with the release of dopamine, a neurotransmitter responsible for feelings of happiness and satisfaction (Müller, 2021). However, this feeling of happiness is fleeting, and soon a renewed desire for the next purchase sets in. This cycle makes consumption a source of short-term gratification that, in the long run, brings neither happiness nor fulfillment.

The mechanism behind this dynamic is deeply embedded in human psychology. Purchasing a product—be it a new piece of clothing, a tech gadget, or a luxurious home accessory—conveys a sense of control and autonomy, which is especially heightened during times of emotional insecurity or overwhelm. The act of buying becomes a symbolic gesture through which people attempt to exert influence over their lives. However, this pursuit of control is deceptive, as consumption merely offers a superficial solution to deeper emotional or social challenges.

In addition to the short-term dopamine release, anticipation also plays a central role. Even the planning and imagining of a purchase activates the brain's reward system. Studies show that the anticipation of acquiring a product is often more intense than the actual joy of ownership (Schmidt, 2019). However, once the product is purchased, this high dissipates, and the brain begins to search for the next goal. This effect, also known as hedonic adaptation, describes the human tendency to quickly get used to new possessions and thus constantly require new stimuli to experience the same level of satisfaction (Frederick & Loewenstein, 1999).

Another important factor is the social component of consumption. In a society where the possession of goods is often equated with status and success, the act of buying is understood not only as an individual decision but also as a means of social communication. Through consumption, people signal belonging to certain groups or distance themselves from others. This behavior is especially amplified in today's world, which is shaped by social media. Platforms like Instagram or TikTok promote a lifestyle based on consumption by propagating images of an apparently perfect life defined by material goods. The pressure to live up to this ideal can lead people to increasingly tie their self-esteem to the possession of certain products.

In doing so, it is often overlooked that the satisfaction achieved through consumption frequently remains an illusion. Emotional needs such as the desire for comfort, recognition, or belonging cannot be sustainably fulfilled by material goods. Instead, a dependency on the constant repetition of the act of buying develops, which in the long term can lead to frustration and inner emptiness. This dynamic is reinforced by societal norms and advertising strategies that portray consumption not only as normal but as essential for a "good life."

Awareness of these mechanisms is a crucial step toward more mindful consumption. The act of buying may be unavoidable in today's world, but reflecting on the underlying emotional needs can help reduce impulsive buying behavior and find more sustainable alternatives. Approaches such as mindfulness and conscious decision-making can help question the emotional triggers of consumption and develop new strategies for need fulfillment.

An additional aspect of shopping addiction is the connection between consumption and social status. In a society strongly shaped by consumption, possessions are often used as a measure of success and recognition. Purchasing certain products signals belonging to a social group or the achievement of a particular standard of living. Social media, in particular, amplifies this effect. Platforms like Instagram and TikTok present an idealized version of consumption, increasing the pressure to gain recognition and validation through the acquisition of specific goods. Studies show that the constant comparison with others on such platforms intensifies consumption pressure and increases the risk of shopping addiction (Kessler & Solomon, 2020).

A real-life example illustrates these mechanisms: Lisa, a young marketing manager, regularly shops online after stressful workdays to reward herself. The moment of purchase gives her a sense of control and satisfaction. But as soon as the goods are delivered, the feeling of happiness fades, and she feels the urge to buy again. Lisa reports feeling trapped in a cycle of short-term relief and persistent craving. This example shows how emotional and cognitive processes can influence consumer behavior and how difficult it is to break out of this cycle.

In addition to the emotional aspects, **cognitive distortions** also play a central role in shopping addiction.

The **hedonic treadmill** effect vividly illustrates why consumption so rarely leads to lasting satisfaction. People not only get used to material possessions but also to the emotional impact of acquisition. The happiness associated with buying a new smartphone, a car, or a luxury watch is limited in intensity and short-lived. This habituation, also called hedonic adaptation, quickly causes the original stimulus to fade, creating the need for a new source of gratification.

A central aspect of this effect is the dynamic that consumers tend to overestimate the long-term emotional impact of a purchase. Psychological studies show that people often believe a particular object or experience will sustainably improve their lives or bring them lasting joy (Wilson & Gilbert, 2005). But as soon as the new product becomes part of everyday life, its emotional value disappears, and attention shifts to the next desirable object. This endless spiral of "wanting more" is not only financially burdensome but can also leave a deep inner emptiness, as it does not truly fulfill the underlying emotional needs.

An example of this is technological progress, especially in the area of smartphones. Consumers often expect that the latest model will bring them more joy through better features or a more innovative design. But once the device is purchased and the initial excitement of the new wears off, the next model is already perceived as more attractive. The advertising industry deliberately reinforces this effect by portraying products as indispensable or revolutionary, drawing consumers into the cycle of constant upgrading and buying (Schneider et al., 2017).

Interestingly, the hedonic treadmill effect is not limited to material goods but can also occur in other areas such as experiences, careers, or relationships. People also get used to positive changes in their lives, whether it's a pay raise, a new car, or even moving to a larger apartment. The initial euphoria quickly gives way to everyday dealings with the new circumstances, and the emotional baseline returns to its original level. This effect is deeply rooted in human psychology, as our brains are programmed to adapt to recurring stimuli in order to use resources efficiently.

The hedonic treadmill effect has far-reaching societal implications. It fosters a culture of overconsumption, as people are constantly searching for new sources of gratification without ever achieving a sense of fulfillment. This dynamic not only drives materialism but also has significant ecological consequences. The production and consumption of ever-new products lead to resource waste and environmental strain. Furthermore, the effect exacerbates social inequalities, as the constant desire for "more" also increases the pressure to keep up with or surpass others, which can lead to tensions, especially in materialistic societies.

> **Important**
>
> Awareness of the hedonic treadmill effect is a key step in questioning consumption patterns. By redefining our expectations of material goods and their significance for our happiness, we can break out of the spiral of constant buying and focus on more sustainable forms of satisfaction.

Reflecting on this effect invites us to seek alternatives to material values, such as focusing on social relationships, personal development, or intangible experiences. In the long term, this not only leads to more conscious consumer behavior but also to deeper and more sustainable satisfaction.

In addition, thought patterns such as the overvaluation of status symbols or the assumption that more expensive products necessarily have higher value or utility come into play. These cognitive distortions are deliberately exploited by marketing strategies that use status, exclusivity, and individual significance as central selling points (Solomon et al., 2019a, b). Advertising messages and branding specifically reinforce the connection between material goods and emotional or social needs. An example of this is the portrayal of luxury brands in the media, which sell not just products but lifestyles. They suggest that acquiring an exclusive product not only enhances one's image but also leads to a more fulfilled and happier life.

These marketing strategies tap into deeply rooted psychological needs, such as the pursuit of social recognition, belonging, or individuality. Those particularly at risk are people who are highly responsive to social comparisons or who have a high degree of uncertainty in their identity. For them, buying an expensive product becomes a symbol of success and appreciation, even if this recognition is only superficial or temporary. The social pressure to acquire such status symbols is further intensified by social media, which idealizes the lives of others and fosters constant comparison. Studies show that social platforms like Instagram or TikTok increase the willingness to make impulsive and status-oriented purchases by staging consumption as a desirable standard (Belk, 2013).

Moreover, the deliberate association of expensive products with prestige and exclusivity leads people to accept irrationally high prices. This behavior is reinforced by the so-called "snob effect," in which the perceived value of a product increases the more expensive or exclusive it is (Leibenstein, 1950). This dynamic is particularly pronounced with luxury goods, whose price is often determined less by actual utility than by their signaling effect. For example, a Rolex watch is not just a timepiece but a symbol of success, wealth, and social superiority. The purchase of such products is motivated not primarily by functional considerations but by the message they are intended to convey to others.

The linkage of consumption with identity and status also has a societal dimension. It reinforces a materialistic worldview in which the value of an individual is increasingly measured by their possessions. This culture of materialism not only fosters social inequalities but also a growing dependence on consumption, as people need ever-new products to maintain or enhance their status. This process often leads to financial overextension, especially among those who try to keep up with higher social strata without having the corresponding means.

Important

Reflecting on these thought patterns and critically engaging with the underlying mechanisms is crucial to breaking the cycle of status-seeking and consumption dependency. A conscious approach to consumption and a focus on non-material values can help achieve greater satisfaction and fulfillment in the long term.

The role of marketing and social influences shows how deeply consumption and luxury addiction are embedded in societal structures. The overvaluation of status symbols and the assumption that higher-priced products are automatically of higher value serve not only as individual drivers but also as engines for economic dynamics that further promote this consumption. A deeper understanding of these mechanisms opens up the possibility of making more critical consumer decisions and developing alternative ways to fulfill needs.

Another factor that intensifies shopping addiction is the constant availability of consumer goods. Online shopping and the use of personalized algorithms promote impulsive buying behavior and make self-control more difficult. Access to credit cards and "buy now, pay later" models also lowers the threshold for purchases that are often not financially sustainable. These technical and economic conditions create an environment that not only enables but actively promotes consumption addiction (Köhler, 2020).

Note

Emotional and cognitive processes often operate subtly but can strongly influence our buying behavior. Awareness of these mechanisms is the first step to breaking them and initiating sustainable change.

The psychology of shopping addiction illustrates how closely emotions, cognitive distortions, and social influences are intertwined. Understanding these mechanisms is crucial for critically questioning one's own consumer behavior and enabling long-term change. At the same time, it becomes clear that shopping addiction is not only an individual but also a societal problem. The focus on consumption as the primary source of happiness and status leads to ecological and social challenges that require a rethinking. In a world strongly shaped by consumption, values such as sustainability, mindfulness, and social responsibility must be strengthened. This section has shown why emotional and cognitive processes are central drivers of shopping addiction and how they can be overcome through reflection and conscious decisions.

Summary

- **Emotional drivers of consumption:** Shopping addiction is based on emotional needs such as comfort, recognition, and stress relief. The act of buying activates the brain's reward system and leads to a short-term release of dopamine, which creates a feeling of happiness. However, this feeling is fleeting, resulting in a cycle of repeated buying that, in the long run, intensifies emotional emptiness and frustration.
- **Cognitive distortions and social influences:** Mechanisms such as the "hedonic treadmill" effect and the "snob effect" cause consumers to overestimate the long-term emotional impact of purchases and associate high-priced products with social status. Advertising and social media reinforce this dynamic by propagating materialistic ideals and increasing the pressure to use consumption as a means of identity formation and social belonging.
- **Societal conditions and consequences:** The constant availability of consumer goods, personalized algorithms, and easy financing options promote impulsive buying behavior and make self-control more difficult. This leads not only to individual problems such as over-indebtedness and dependency but also to ecological and social challenges. Critical reflection on these mechanisms is key to developing more sustainable consumption patterns and fostering greater social responsibility.

2.3 Consumption as a Substitute: When Shopping Is Meant to Fill the Soul

Example

In this section, you will learn how consumption serves as compensation for inner emptiness and social deficits, the mechanisms underlying this behavior, and the long-term consequences for individuals and society.

The act of consuming has evolved in our modern society from a mere necessity to an emotionally charged ritual. Shopping is no longer just a response to needs such as food, clothing, or shelter, but is often used as a substitute to fill emotional and social voids. In doing so, consumption serves a seemingly simple but deceptive function: it promises short-term relief in moments of loneliness, stress, or self-doubt. But how sustainable is this effect, and what dynamics underlie it?

Consumption often serves as a short-term compensation for negative feelings. When inner emptiness, boredom, or emotional strain arise, many people reach for their wallets or fill virtual shopping carts. The psychological explanation for this lies in the activation of the brain's reward system. The act of buying triggers the release of dopamine, a neurotransmitter associated with pleasure and satisfaction (Schmidt, 2019). But this effect is short-lived. The feeling of fulfillment quickly disappears, leaving behind a void that is often greater than before. This pattern leads to a vicious cycle in which consumption is repeatedly used as a remedy for inner dissatisfaction.

The short-term relief created by the act of buying is comparable to other behaviors aimed at immediate reward, such as emotional eating, excessive media consumption, or gambling. In these moments, the long-term perspective fades into the background, and satisfying the immediate need becomes the priority. Studies show that this dynamic occurs especially in people who have difficulty regulating their emotions or developing alternative coping strategies (Hirschman, 1992). Consumption then becomes a seemingly simple and readily available solution that, however, does not solve the underlying problems but rather exacerbates them.

The negative reinforcement provided by the act of buying—that is, the short-term alleviation of stress or dissatisfaction—masks the real issue. People who repeatedly resort to this strategy become accustomed to regulating their emotions through consumption. This not only leads to financial difficulties but can also intensify feelings of helplessness. The inner emptiness that was briefly filled by the act of buying is often experienced afterward as even more intense. Feelings of guilt, shame, or the realization that the purchased object offers no lasting value exacerbate the emotional burden.

Another problem arises when consumption serves as a substitute for social or emotional bonds. People who suffer from loneliness or have difficulty forming genuine interpersonal connections often seek comfort or belonging in the act of buying. The acquisition of consumer goods is then perceived not just as an act of need fulfillment but as a kind of self-care that, however, remains superficial. This is particularly problematic when consumption becomes a habit, as those affected become increasingly less able to find other, more sustainable forms of emotional regulation.

Digitalization and the availability of online shopping intensify this phenomenon. The quick access to consumer goods around the clock, the constant presence of personalized advertising, and the ability to complete purchases with just a few clicks make it easier than ever to consume impulsively. This not only lowers the threshold but also reinforces the feeling that consumption offers an immediate solution to emotional problems. The brain learns to prefer these quick rewards, further increasing dependence on consumption (Belk, 2013). In the long run, this behavior leads to an alienation from the original purpose of consumption. Originally, the acquisition of goods served to meet concrete needs and improve quality of life. But when consumption is used to compensate for negative feelings, it loses its original function and becomes an act of self-deception. Instead of real fulfillment, only the pursuit of the next reward remains—a vicious cycle that not only burdens mental health but also has social and financial consequences.

> **Important**
>
> Understanding these mechanisms is a first step toward breaking the vicious cycle of compensatory consumption. It requires both reflection on one's own needs and the development of alternative strategies for emotion regulation to bring about long-term change.

A vivid example is provided by Thomas, a 45-year-old management consultant who reports a full schedule and constant pressure to succeed. After long workdays, he regularly orders expensive gadgets or clothing online. For a brief moment, the purchase gives him a sense of control over his life and of doing something good for himself. But by the next morning, he feels just as stressed as before. His purchases do not solve the underlying problems but rather exacerbate them through increasing financial strain.

In addition to emotional reasons, the social dimension of consumption plays a decisive role. Consumption is often used to demonstrate belonging and social status. Especially in a world dominated by social media, the purchase of goods has a performative component. Platforms like Instagram or TikTok reinforce this trend by presenting consumption as a central part of a successful lifestyle. This social pressure can lead people to consume more and more in order to gain recognition and validation. However, instead of genuine social connections, only superficial bonds are formed, which can intensify the feeling of isolation in the long term (Baumeister & Leary, 1995).

Cultural factors also contribute to the use of consumption as a substitute for inner needs. Western consumer culture has placed material values at the pinnacle of the promise of happiness. "Having" is often equated with "being," and the value of an individual is increasingly measured by their possessions. These values are continuously reinforced by advertising, media, and marketing strategies. As Kasser (2002) shows, however, this focus on material goals leads to lower life satisfaction and an increased risk of psychological distress.

> **Important**
>
> Recognizing that consumption does not provide a sustainable solution for emotional and social problems is crucial for developing alternative strategies for need fulfillment. Mindfulness and strengthening social bonds can help break the cycle of compensatory consumption.

The long-term consequences of consumption as a substitute strategy are far-reaching both individually and societally. On an individual level, this behavior often leads to feelings of guilt, shame, and a growing inner emptiness, which is intensified by the constant search for fulfillment. The risk of over-indebtedness also increases, further impairing quality of life. On a societal level, this behavior contributes to environmental destruction, social inequality, and a culture of overproduction. The Earth's resources are being exploited at an unsustainable rate, and the social costs of consumerism are being shifted to future generations.

> **Reference to Exercise 3**
>
> In Sect. 9.3.3 "Reflection on Concrete Consumption Behavior," you will find a practical exercise to help you analyze your specific consumption patterns and identify the emotional and social triggers behind your buying behavior. You will learn how to develop alternative strategies to approach consumption more consciously and sustainably in the long term.

> **Summary**
>
> - **Psychological mechanisms of consumption:** Consumption is often used as a coping strategy to compensate for emotional deficits such as inner emptiness, stress, or insecurity. The act of buying activates the brain's reward system and produces short-term gratification, which quickly fades and reinforces the cycle of addictive behavior.
> - **Social and cultural influences:** Consumption serves not only individual purposes but is also used to demonstrate social status or belonging. Advertising, social media, and cultural norms promote a consumer culture in which the value of the individual is increasingly measured by possessions and material achievements, intensifying the pressure to overconsume.
> - **Long-term consequences and solutions:** The persistent use of consumption as a substitute for emotional and social needs leads to feelings of guilt, financial problems, and a heightened sense of isolation. On a societal level, excessive consumption contributes to environmental destruction and social

> inequality. Long-term solutions require reflection on individual consumption patterns, strengthening social bonds, and developing sustainable alternatives for need fulfillment.
>
> Consumption as a substitute for emotional and social needs is a widespread phenomenon that may bring short-term relief but is not sustainable in the long run, either individually or societally. Reflecting on the underlying mechanisms and seeking alternative strategies for need fulfillment are essential steps to breaking this cycle.

References

Baumeister, R. F., & Leary, M. R. (1995). The need to belong: Desire for interpersonal attachments as a fundamental human motivation. *Psychological Bulletin, 117*(3), 497–529.

Belk, R. W. (2013). Extended self in a digital world. *Journal of Consumer Research, 40*(3), 477–500.

Hirschman, E. C. (1992). The consciousness of addiction: Toward a general theory of compulsive consumption. *Journal of Consumer Research, 19*(2), 155–179.

Kasser, T. (2002). *The high price of materialism*. MIT Press.

Kessler, R. C., & Solomon, S. D. (2020). The influence of social media on consumer behavior. *Journal of Psychological Studies, 15*(4), 120–136.

Köhler, M. (2020). *Kaufsucht und Gesellschaft: Eine psychologische Analyse*. Springer.

Leibenstein, H. (1950). Bandwagon, snob, and veblen effects in the theory of consumers' demand. *The Quarterly Journal of Economics, 64*(2), 183–207.

Müller, S. (2021). *Die Psychologie des Kaufens: Warum wir Dinge wollen, die wir nicht brauchen*. Hanser.

Schmidt, L. (2019). *Neuropsychologie des Konsums: Wie unser Gehirn den Markt formt*. Beltz.

Schneider, T., Belk, R., & Holbrook, M. B. (2017). Consumer responses to technological evolution. *Journal of Consumer Research, 44*(2), 329–345.

Solomon, M. R., Bamossy, G. J., Askegaard, S., & Hogg, M. K. (2019a). *Consumer behaviour: A European perspective*. Pearson Education Limited.

Solomon, M. R., Bamossy, G., & Askegaard, S. (2019b). *Consumer behavior: A European perspective*. Pearson Education.

Wilson, T. D., & Gilbert, D. T. (2005). Affective forecasting: Knowing what to want. *Current Directions in Psychological Science, 14*(3), 131–134.

3

Self-Diagnosis and Reflection

Abstract This chapter presents methods for self-analysis that enable the early identification of problematic consumption patterns. Checklists and reflection questions help to examine personal purchasing motives and to determine whether excessive consumption may be compensating for emotional or social deficits. In addition, the chapter explores which psychological and societal factors influence consumer decisions. The chapter invites the reader to critically reflect on their previous purchasing habits and to take initial steps toward more conscious decision-making.

Change begins with self-awareness. Chap. 3 is dedicated to the question of how you can critically examine your own consumption behavior in order to recognize early signs of consumption and luxury addiction. With the help of practical exercises and checklists, this chapter offers you the opportunity to delve deeper into your own motives and patterns. It lays the foundation for change by creating awareness of problematic behaviors while also providing tools to analyze them. Reflection is the key to better understanding your relationship with consumption and taking the first step toward a more conscious life.

© The Author(s), under exclusive license to Springer-Verlag GmbH, DE, part of Springer Nature 2026

O. Hoffmann, *Rethink Consumption*, https://doi.org/10.1007/978-3-662-72946-5_3

3.1   Am I at Risk? Early Signs of Consumption Problems

> **Example**
>
> In this section, you will learn how to recognize typical warning signs of consumption or luxury addiction and why early reflection on your behavior is crucial to avoid long-term problems.

In a world where consumption is omnipresent, it initially seems difficult to distinguish between normal and problematic buying behavior. But as with any addiction, there are clear warning signs in consumption and luxury addiction that can indicate a creeping dependency. Often, the problem begins subtly, almost imperceptibly: an occasional impulse purchase that seems harmless, a "reward purchase" after a stressful day, or the feeling of needing to own something to feel more complete or better. Yet these very behaviors can be signs that consumption is no longer just about meeting needs, but is being used as a means of coping with emotional or social tensions.

A key warning sign is loss of control. When the urge to buy takes over and rational thinking is pushed aside, this can indicate the onset of consumption problems. A practical example is Melanie, a 29-year-old teacher who regularly shops online. At first, it was occasional orders, but now she spends hours every day browsing offers and spends far more money than she can afford. She tries to hide her spending from her partner and often feels guilty after making a purchase. This feeling of guilt, combined with an inability to stop the behavior, is a common sign that consumption has become problematic.

Another indicator is emotional reactions to the act of buying. Consumers who use shopping as a way to regulate stress, boredom, or inner emptiness often report a brief high during the purchase, followed by disappointment or regret. These emotional fluctuations are typical of addictive behavior and can be a sign that consumption has become a coping strategy. Studies show that people who tend toward impulsive buying behavior often have difficulty regulating their emotions in other ways (Kasser, 2002).

In addition to emotional and financial aspects, social warning signs are also crucial. When consumption habits lead to strained relationships because those affected hide their spending or devote most of their time to shopping, this is a serious red flag. Consumption can become increasingly isolating as those affected fixate on their purchases and neglect social interactions or activities.

Reflecting on these signs is the first step in recognizing and addressing consumption problems. A simple test is to ask yourself questions such as: "Do I buy things I don't really need?", "Do I spend more money than I want or can afford?" or "Do I use shopping to make myself feel better?" Such self-tests can help identify patterns and raise awareness of your own behavior.

> **Important**
>
> Early detection of consumption problems can prevent the behavior from developing into an addiction. It is helpful to be honest with yourself and, if necessary, seek support.

The consequences of ignored warning signs can be far-reaching. Financial problems, psychological burdens such as anxiety and depression, and social isolation are among the most common consequences of consumption problems. But with the right approach—through reflection, self-tests, and professional support—these developments can be prevented or reversed. Confronting your own consumption habits is not only a sign of self-care but also an important step toward a more conscious, sustainable lifestyle (Baumeister & Leary, 1995).

> **Summary**
>
> This section has shown how you can recognize typical warning signs of consumption problems. By paying attention to emotional, financial, and social cues, you can take early action and avoid long-term consequences. Awareness and reflection are the keys to a healthy relationship with consumption.

3.2 Why do We Buy What We Buy? A Self-Assessment

> **Example**
>
> In this section, you will learn how personal consumption patterns develop, what motivations influence our buying behavior, and how you can better understand them.

Our buying behavior is shaped by a multitude of conscious and unconscious influences that go far beyond mere necessity. Why do we choose a particular product when we could have chosen a cheaper alternative? Why do we buy things we don't really need? These questions lead us to the underlying psychological, social, and cultural dynamics that govern our consumption behavior. Becoming aware of these processes is the first step to reflecting on and, if necessary, reshaping our decisions.

Buying is rarely just a rational act. Studies show that emotional needs play a central role. Whether it's joy, stress management, or the need for recognition—our consumption decisions are often an attempt to fulfill these inner desires. A particularly striking example is the choice of a status symbol such as an expensive watch or a luxury car. These purchases are less about the functionality of the products and more about the social signal they send. At the same time, there are purchases that arise from the desire to reward oneself or escape emotional emptiness. However, the joy of buying is often short-lived, which drives many people into a cycle of buying and dissatisfaction.

Another central factor influencing our consumption behavior is social comparison. In a world dominated by social media, we are confronted daily with the staging of lifestyles that are often linked to consumption. These portrayals awaken in us the desire to keep up and reinforce the feeling that our happiness depends on certain products. But comparing ourselves to others is a double-edged sword: while it can motivate us to improve our standard of living, it also leads to dissatisfaction when we cannot afford what others have. This is where reflection comes in: What value do these purchases really have for our lives? And what needs are we trying to satisfy with them?

In addition to emotional and social influences, there are also deeply rooted cultural imprints that shape our consumption patterns. In Western societies, the link between success and material possessions is particularly strong. Advertising and marketing reinforce this connection and present consumption as a path to happiness and fulfillment. At the same time, modern business models such as "Buy now, pay later" or personalized recommendations promote impulsive buying behavior, making it harder to critically engage with our needs. Examining these dynamics can help us become more aware of the role of consumption in our lives and break free from externally imposed patterns (Dittmar, 2008).

A practical example can illustrate this process of reflection. Lena, a 28-year-old student, describes how she often buys clothes even though her wardrobe is already overflowing. "I know I don't really need it, but in the moment it feels right," she says. An analysis of her buying behavior showed that she often shops during stressful periods to calm herself or distract herself. Through this realization, Lena began to question her behavior and look for alternatives to cope with stress, such as exercise or meditation.

> **Important**
>
> The key to more conscious consumption decisions lies in reflection. By recognizing your own motivations and patterns, you can free yourself from unconscious impulses and develop more sustainable buying behavior.

Self-assessing your consumption patterns is a first step toward breaking out of automated behaviors. However, this process requires honesty and patience. A helpful approach is to keep a consumption diary in which you note what you bought, why you bought it, and how you felt about it. This method can provide valuable insights and reveal patterns that you were previously unaware of.

> **Summary**
>
> Our buying behavior is driven by a variety of emotional, social, and cultural influences. This section has shown how important it is to recognize and critically question these patterns in order to consume more consciously and sustainably in the long term. Reflecting on your motivations is the key to a new relationship with consumption.

3.3 Checklists for Identifying Consumption and Luxury Addiction

> **Example**
>
> In this section, you will learn how to reflect on your own consumption behavior and use practical checklists to better assess the risks of consumption and luxury addiction.

Reflecting on your own buying behavior is the first step in finding out whether this behavior is problematic or even addictive. In a world flooded with consumption stimuli, it is difficult to draw clear boundaries between healthy consumption and excessive buying behavior. Checklists offer a simple yet effective way to question yourself and recognize problematic patterns. They are not only a tool for diagnosis but also a foundation for change.

A central feature of consumption addiction is loss of control. Many affected individuals report that they are unable to control their urge to buy, even when they are aware of the negative consequences.

> **Note**
>
> A comprehensive compilation of checklists covering all aspects of buying and luxury addiction can be found in Sect. 9.2.

An example illustrates the relevance of such checklists: Laura, a 29-year-old student, noticed that she was buying clothes more and more often, even though she didn't need them. A checklist helped her analyze her spending. She found that she regularly shopped to calm herself after stressful days and often exceeded her financial limits. This insight was the starting point for her to make more conscious decisions and develop strategies for impulse control.

Identifying luxury addiction, on the other hand, requires a different approach. Here, the focus is less on the buying impulse and more on the targeted investment in high-priced goods that serve as status symbols. Questions such as "Do you buy certain products to impress others?" or "Do you feel less valuable without luxury goods?" can help to question the influence of social pressure and one's own orientation toward status. Luxury addiction is often subtler than consumption addiction, as it is socially accepted or even admired, making self-recognition more difficult.

> **Practical Tip**
>
> Take the time to fill out the checklists in Sect. 9.2 honestly and without self-judgment. They are not a test to pass, but a tool to better understand yourself and take the first steps toward change.

Scientific studies show that such self-assessment tools are a valuable aid in raising people's awareness of their behavioral patterns (Müller, 2021). They not only encourage engagement with one's own consumption behavior but also lay the foundation for further steps, such as developing a more conscious approach to money and resources.

Summary and Classification of the Checklists

The checklists in this section are valuable tools for systematically reflecting on your own consumption behavior, identifying problematic patterns, and initiating targeted steps toward change. Each checklist focuses on a specific aspect of consumption addiction and helps develop a comprehensive understanding of the underlying mechanisms and their effects.

1. Self-Awareness through Reflection

The checklists begin with general questions about consumption addiction and guide the user through a structured self-assessment. This process helps to make unconscious behavioral patterns visible, such as impulsive buying, emotional triggers, and financial burdens. Writing down the answers encourages engagement with one's own behavior and makes it easier to identify problematic tendencies.

2. Emotional and Cognitive Mechanisms

A central focus is on the emotional and cognitive factors that drive consumption addiction. The checklists on emotional triggers and cognitive distortions deepen the understanding of how stress, loneliness, or irrational beliefs lead to uncontrolled buying behavior. By making these mechanisms conscious, the user lays the foundation for targeted work on their challenges.

3. Practical Interventions and Strategies

The checklists for coping and change offer concrete, actionable approaches to regulate consumption behavior in the long term. These include both preventive measures, such as avoiding triggers, and active strategies to strengthen impulse control and emotional resilience. For those who have difficulty making changes on their own, additional support options such as professional help or self-help groups are suggested.

4. Differentiated Consideration of Aspects

Dividing into specific topics such as self-esteem, financial burden, or social impact enables a differentiated analysis of consumption addiction. This allows those affected to work specifically on the factors that are particularly relevant to them. This modularity of the checklists supports both the individual adaptation of reflection and a focused intervention.

5. Integration and Further Development

The checklists build on each other and thus offer a logical development process: from initial self-awareness to the analysis of underlying mechanisms to the implementation of sustainable strategies. This structured approach enables those affected to regain control over their consumption behavior before it leads to serious financial, social, or psychological consequences.

In summary, the checklists offer not only a means of self-diagnosis but also a clear framework for action to cope with consumption addiction. They promote self-reflection, create awareness of the emotional and cognitive backgrounds, and provide practical approaches to regain control over one's own behavior. By guiding the user from insight to change, the checklists are a central component of prevention and intervention in consumption addiction.

> **Important**
>
> Checklists are not a substitute for professional diagnosis. If the results indicate a pronounced consumption or luxury addiction, you should consider seeking professional advice.

The aim of this section is to provide you with tools to critically question your behavior. The checklists are intended not only to highlight problems but also to provide food for thought for developing alternatives. They are a first step toward shaping your relationship with consumption more consciously and bringing about positive change in the long term.

> **Summary**
>
> This section has shown how checklists can serve as a practical tool to identify problematic behavioral patterns and take the first step toward more conscious consumption behavior. An honest engagement with these questions can help you gain greater clarity about your relationship with consumption.

References

Baumeister, R. F., & Leary, M. R. (1995). The Need to Belong: Desire for Interpersonal Attachments as a Fundamental Human Motivation. *Psychological Bulletin, 117*(3), 497–529.

Dittmar, H. (2008). *Consumer culture, identity, and well-being: The search for the "Good Life" and the "Body Perfect"*. Psychology Press.

Kahneman, D. (2011). *Thinking, fast and slow*. Farrar, Straus and Giroux.

Kasser, T. (2002). *The high price of materialism*. MIT Press.

Müller, S. (2021). *Die Psychologie des Kaufens: Warum wir Dinge wollen, die wir nicht brauchen*. Hanser.

4

The Causes of Addiction

Abstract The causes of consumerism and luxury addiction are multifaceted. This chapter analyzes individual risk factors such as personality traits, emotional instability, and lack of impulse control. The influence of external factors—particularly advertising, social media, and societal consumption norms—is also critically examined. The chapter highlights how digital platforms create personalized purchase incentives to entice consumers into ever-increasing consumption frequency. Furthermore, it addresses how deeply cultural narratives of prosperity and material security are embedded in our self-concept and foster compulsive buying behavior.

What drives people to lose control over their consumption behavior? Chap. 4 is dedicated to the deeper causes of consumption and luxury addiction. From individual personality traits and psychological risk factors to the powerful influences of advertising, social media, and cultural norms, this chapter sheds light on the diverse mechanisms that promote excessive buying behavior. The aim is to understand the complex interplay between internal vulnerabilities and external dynamics in order to identify the roots of addiction and foster a more conscious approach to consumption in the long term.

O. Hoffmann, *Rethink Consumption*, https://doi.org/10.1007/978-3-662-72946-5_4

4.1 Personality Traits and Individual Risk Factors

> **Example**
>
> In this section, you will learn which personality traits and psychological factors make people more susceptible to consumption addiction, and how these characteristics interact with social and cultural influences.

Susceptibility to consumption addiction is significantly shaped by individual personality traits and psychological factors. While external influences such as advertising or social media reinforce consumption behavior, certain character traits and coping strategies create an internal foundation that makes people more receptive to problematic consumption. It is these internal factors that determine whether someone can resist a consumption stimulus or falls into a cycle of impulsive buying and negative consequences.

A key factor highlighted in numerous studies is impulsivity. People with high impulsivity often make decisions without long-term planning or reflection. The spontaneous purchase of a product serves as an immediate reward that temporarily masks negative feelings such as stress or boredom. This "instant gratification" is supported by the activation of the brain's reward system, particularly through the release of dopamine, which conveys a sense of pleasure and satisfaction (Müller, 2021). However, this effect is short-lived, and the underlying problems—be it emotional stress, loneliness, or dissatisfaction—remain. The lack of self-control often leads to purchases that are unconsidered, financially burdensome, and ultimately counterproductive (Rook, 1987).

This behavioral pattern is significantly reinforced by the modern consumer environment. The constant availability of products, especially through online shopping, plays a central role in promoting impulsive buying decisions. Platforms like Amazon or Zalando have reduced the purchasing process to just a few clicks, lowering the threshold for spontaneous decisions. Features such as "Buy with one click" or personalized product suggestions increase the temptation by speeding up the purchasing process and creating the impression that the desired product is just a moment away (Haws & Poynor, 2008). The ease and speed with which purchases can be completed leave little room for reflection or consideration of consequences. An additional reinforcing factor is the psychological impact of advertising incentives and sales strategies. Time-limited offers, such as "Available today only" or "Only 3 left in stock," create artificial pressure and promote impulsive behavior. These tactics exploit so-called loss aversion—the tendency to feel losses more strongly than gains, leading people to act immediately rather than miss out on a perceived deal (Tversky & Kahneman, 1991). For impulsive buyers, this can have a particularly strong effect, as they are already more prone to emotional decisions.

The shift of consumption into the digital realm has also intensified social comparisons, which likewise promote impulsive behavior. On social media platforms like Instagram or TikTok, consumer goods are often presented in an idealized way. Influencers and advertising campaigns convey the impression that owning certain products is synonymous with success, attractiveness, or happiness. People with high impulsivity are especially receptive to such messages, as they are more likely to act spontaneously and respond more strongly to emotional stimuli (Vohs & Faber, 2007). The purchase of a promoted product is perceived as a kind of "quick fix" to emulate the portrayed ideal. In addition to external influences, individual emotion regulation ability also plays a crucial role. People who have difficulty coping with negative feelings often use impulsive purchases as a coping strategy. The act of buying provides a short-term sense of control and relief, which quickly fades. Studies show that this "self-medicative" use of consumption can lead to even greater emotional distress in the long run, as the financial consequences create additional stress and reinforce the sense of loss of control (Hirschman, 1992).

> **Important**
>
> Impulsivity alone does not necessarily lead to consumption addiction. Rather, problematic buying behavior arises from the interplay of personality traits such as impulsivity with external factors like marketing strategies, social pressure, and the constant availability of products. Conscious reflection and the development of alternative strategies for emotion regulation are crucial steps to break this cycle.

Another decisive characteristic is low self-esteem. Individuals with a fragile self-image often try to define their worth through the possession of material goods. Buying a new car, a designer handbag, or a tech gadget gives them a sense of social recognition and success. But this feeling is usually short-lived, as the underlying problem—low self-esteem—is not resolved (Dittmar, 2008). An example illustrates this dynamic: Sabine, a 38-year-old management consultant, describes how she buys expensive clothes after professional setbacks to appear confident in front of colleagues. "It makes me feel good, but deep down I know it doesn't really help," she says. Her behavior shows how strongly the need for recognition and the avoidance of weakness can influence consumption.

Emotional sensitivity and a high level of perceived stress also contribute to susceptibility to consumption addiction. People who have difficulty dealing with negative emotions such as anxiety, sadness, or uncertainty often develop strategies to suppress these feelings in the short term. The act of buying becomes a seemingly simple means to reduce inner tension and experience relief for a moment. Scientific studies show that this mechanism is closely linked to the activation of the brain's reward system. As soon as a product is purchased, the brain releases dopamine, which provides a short-term feeling of satisfaction and control. But this effect is fleeting. Once the high subsides, the original negative emotions return, often intensified by feelings of guilt over the uncontrolled purchase.

A practical example illustrates this dynamic: Sarah, a 42-year-old teacher, describes how she regularly browses stores or online shops for products to "cheer herself up" after a stressful day. "I buy things I don't really need, just to feel better for a moment," she says. But as soon as the purchases are made, she feels dissatisfied and starts blaming herself. This cycle of stress, impulsive buying, and subsequent guilt leads to increased inner restlessness. Sarah's story shows how consumption as a coping strategy not only leaves emotional problems unresolved but often creates additional emotional strain. The problem is that while the act of buying is perceived as relief in the short term, the underlying causes of emotional stress are not addressed. People who use consumption as a coping strategy often avoid directly confronting their feelings or the situations that trigger them. Consumption thus becomes an avoidance behavior that weakens emotional resilience and increases dependence on external stimuli (Hirschman, 1992). The long-term consequences of this behavior are often severe. The constant attempt to compensate for emotional or social deficits through consumption can lead to financial problems, social isolation, and an intensification of the original negative feelings. In addition, those affected often lack a sustainable strategy for emotion regulation, which further increases dependence on consumption. To break this cycle, a conscious engagement with one's own emotions and needs is required. Techniques such as mindfulness or targeted exercises to build emotional resilience can help find alternative ways to cope with stress and negative feelings.

> **Important**
>
> The key to change lies in reflecting on the underlying emotional needs and developing sustainable strategies for emotion regulation. Consumption can provide short-term relief, but real solutions require a deeper engagement with the causes of emotional distress.

A central aspect related to the characteristics mentioned is the need for social belonging. In a materialistic society, consumption is often used as a means to signal belonging or to distinguish oneself from others. People who are highly responsive to social comparisons are particularly susceptible to the pressure to strengthen their social position by purchasing branded products or status symbols. This consumption mechanism is based on the so-called "symbolic capital," a concept that describes how material possessions are interpreted as signs of status and prestige in social interactions (Bourdieu, 1984).

Studies show that this pressure is significantly intensified by social media, as platforms like Instagram, TikTok, or Facebook promote the portrayal of a "perfect" lifestyle (Belk, 2013). On social media, images of luxury goods, exotic trips, and elaborately staged everyday moments are not only shared but often idealized and admired. This visual and emotional enhancement of consumption reinforces the perception that material possessions are not only desirable but essential for happiness and success. Particularly problematic is that social media creates a constant opportunity for comparison. Users not only see the consumption of their acquaintances but also the staged lifestyles of influencers and celebrities, who often set unattainable standards.

This social pressure particularly affects young people whose identities are still being formed. During adolescence, social recognition plays a central role, and the desire for belonging is often expressed through external markers such as clothing, technology, or other status symbols. Adolescents are strongly influenced by peer groups and the cultural ideals conveyed to them by the media. Studies show that adolescents who spend a lot of time on social media are at higher risk of adopting materialistic values and using them as the basis for their self-esteem (Chaplin & John, 2007). This behavior can drive them into a cycle of excessive consumption and dissatisfaction, as fulfillment through consumption is only temporary.

> **Reference to Exercise 4**
>
> You will find this exercise in Sect. 9.3.4 "Reflection on Personal Consumption Triggers." It is particularly helpful for identifying the emotional and situational triggers for your consumption behavior. It provides a foundation for developing targeted measures to reduce impulsive purchases and to manage your consumption more consciously in the long term.

But it is not only adolescents who are affected. Adults are also subject to the influence of social comparisons. In professional contexts or social networks, it is often expected that certain standards are met—whether through clothing, technical devices, or lifestyle. These expectations create subtle but lasting pressure, increasing the willingness to spend money on products or services that are less functional and more symbolic in nature. This mechanism is also noticeable in the workplace, where the possession of certain items—from designer clothing to luxury cars—is perceived as an indicator of professional success.

Social media and the associated consumer culture reinforce this pressure by generating an endless stream of images and messages that support the notion that happiness and success are inextricably linked to the acquisition of goods. This idealization of materialistic values not only promotes excessive consumption but also contributes to the development of a mental dependency in which self-worth and social recognition are strongly tied to possessions. The constant availability of consumer goods and the ease of online shopping further help to maintain this mechanism.

> **Important**
>
> Unreflective adoption of consumption as a means of social belonging not only reinforces individual dependencies but also contributes to societal and ecological problems. A conscious approach to the mechanisms of social media and the dynamics of social comparison is essential to counteract this pressure.

The combination of internal and external factors shows that consumption addiction has a complex dynamic. Individual character traits provide the foundation, while social and cultural influences such as constant access to consumer goods and the idealization of materialism reinforce this tendency. Preventive strategies should therefore address not only individual weaknesses but also question the societal conditions that promote this behavior.

> **Important**
>
> Personality traits such as impulsivity or low self-esteem do not automatically make people addicted. Rather, problematic behavioral patterns often arise from the interplay of these traits with external factors such as social norms or advertising messages. Conscious reflection can help break these mechanisms.

Summary

- **Individual personality traits as the basis of consumption addiction:** Personality traits such as impulsivity, low self-esteem, and emotional sensitivity increase susceptibility to consumption addiction. These characteristics promote impulsive buying behavior, which often serves as a coping strategy for negative emotions such as stress, anxiety, or uncertainty, but does not provide a sustainable solution.
- **External influences and social dynamics:** Social media, advertising, and the constant availability of consumer goods reinforce addictive behavior. Advertising strategies and idealized lifestyles on social media promote materialistic values and suggest that happiness and success can be achieved through consumption. Adolescents and people with a high need for comparison are particularly susceptible to this social pressure.
- **The complex interplay between internal and external factors:** Consumption addiction arises from the interaction of individual weaknesses and societal conditions. Preventive approaches must therefore aim both to promote emotional resilience and self-reflection and to critically question societal dynamics such as the idealization of materialism. A conscious approach to consumption stimuli can help break the cycle of addictive behavior.

This section has shown how personality traits such as impulsivity, low self-esteem, and emotional sensitivity increase susceptibility to consumption addiction. Understanding these factors is crucial for developing preventive measures and reducing the influence of external consumption stimuli.

4.2 The Influence of Advertising, Social Media, and Digital Consumption

> **Example**
>
> In this section, you will learn how companies use manipulative strategies to deliberately influence our buying behavior, and how these mechanisms shape our thinking and actions.

Advertising and social media are omnipresent. Every minute of our daily lives, we are confronted with messages, images, and videos designed to make products and services appealing to us. However, these messages are not random, but the result of highly developed psychological and technological strategies aimed at capturing our attention, arousing our needs, and ultimately steering our buying behavior. Digital consumption amplifies this influence by using personalized data to present us with exactly what we seem to want at the right moment.

A main aspect of this manipulation is the use of emotional and psychological levers. Advertising aims not only to sell products but to create feelings. It evokes desires for happiness, recognition, or belonging, which are supposedly associated with the purchase of certain products. For example, an advertisement for a luxury car not only highlights the vehicle's advantages but also conveys a sense of success and status. Studies show that this emotional charge of consumer goods has a significant impact on our behavior, as it appeals to our subconscious and often bypasses rational considerations (Belk, 2013).

Social media have revolutionized these mechanisms. Platforms like Instagram, Facebook, and TikTok use algorithms that not only analyze our consumption behavior but actively influence it. They show us targeted content that captures our attention and intensifies our desire for social comparison. Influencers play a key role in this. By presenting products seemingly authentically in their everyday lives, they create an emotional connection that traditional advertising often cannot achieve. One example is Anna, a young mother who regularly promotes children's clothing products on Instagram. Her followers trust her because they feel like part of her life. The products she recommends are not only bought because they seem useful, but because they create a connection to Anna.

This form of manipulation is particularly effective because it penetrates deeply into our psychological need structure. People have a fundamental need for belonging and social recognition (Baumeister & Leary, 1995). By specifically addressing these needs, social media increase the pressure to become part of a supposedly ideal lifestyle through consumption. The products presented by influencers are not just consumer goods, but symbols of a life that many of their followers aspire to. This makes the advertising more subtle but also more effective, as it is based on social relationships that are perceived as authentic in the digital world.

At the same time, the combination of advertising and algorithmic data analysis has reached a new level of audience specificity. Platforms not only analyze which products we buy, but also how we feel and how we behave in certain contexts. This information is used to show us personalized advertising that addresses our current needs or emotional states. A study by Zuboff (2019) shows how these "surveillance capitalism" techniques can not only predict our behavior but actively shape it. For example, if a user searches more frequently for relaxation products after a stressful week, they may be shown targeted ads for wellness vacations or luxury spa treatments. Such tailored content amplifies the effect of advertising and makes it harder for consumers to resist these impulses. In addition, these mechanisms shape cultural norms. Consumption is no longer just a personal decision but is presented as a social imperative. Those who do not own or consume certain products risk being excluded from the social fabric. This creates consumption compulsions that not only influence individual behavior but also shape societal discourse. This effect is particularly pronounced in younger generations, as social media have established comparison with others as a daily ritual. This leads to a constant competition for status and recognition, which is played out through the purchase of products.

> **Important**
>
> Recognizing how profoundly advertising and social media influence our consumption behavior is a crucial step toward dealing more consciously with these mechanisms. Mindfulness and critical thinking can help to arm oneself against subtle manipulations and make more sustainable decisions.

The long-term effects of these developments are felt both individually and societally. Individuals increasingly suffer from the pressure to define their identity and social value through the possession of certain goods. At the same time, these dynamics exacerbate social inequalities, as not everyone has the financial means to keep up with consumption standards. On a societal level, the constant promotion of consumption leads to overproduction of goods and massive environmental strain. Advertising and social media are not only drivers but also amplifiers of this problem.

Another dimension of digital consumption is personalization. E-commerce platforms like Amazon or Zalando use extensive data to suggest products that match our preferences and previous purchasing decisions. These personalized recommendations are designed to trigger buying impulses. Particularly effective is the technique of scarcity, where it is indicated that a product is "only a few left in stock." These messages create the feeling of missing a unique opportunity, which increases our buying pressure. Such techniques are based on psychological principles such as the so-called loss aversion effect, which describes that we feel losses more strongly than gains (Kahneman & Tversky, 1979). In addition, personalization is reinforced by so-called algorithmic nudges. These algorithms analyze not only our purchase history but also our online behavior, such as the time spent on certain product pages or search queries. Based on this data, tailored recommendations are created that precisely address our individual preferences. Such nudges are particularly effective because they create the feeling that the suggested products have been selected especially for us. This targeted approach not only increases the likelihood of a purchase but also strengthens the emotional bond to the platform. The consumer feels understood and recognized, which in turn lowers the threshold for impulsive buying. Another frequently used principle is the social proof phenomenon, which is also strongly anchored in digital consumption. Platforms present ratings, customer reviews, and bestseller lists to influence the buyer's decision. The idea that other people rate or frequently buy a particular product positively conveys security and increases the attractiveness of that product. Social media and influencer marketing have particularly reinforced this effect by presenting the consumption of certain products as a desirable status symbol. Through these mechanisms, the act of buying is not only rationally justified but also emotionally charged. The psychological impact of these strategies is further enhanced by gamification elements. Many platforms reward us with virtual points, discounts, or exclusive offers when we shop more frequently. Such mechanisms promote the desire for repeated buying behavior by activating the brain's reward system. The purchase is thus no longer perceived merely as a transaction but as part of a game in which the goal is to collect rewards and maximize supposed advantages. This dynamic can be particularly problematic for people with a high tendency toward impulsive behavior or low self-control, as they are more strongly encouraged to consume by such mechanisms.

The combination of personalization, scarcity, social proof, and gamification creates a highly stimulating consumer experience based on the basic principles of behavioral psychology. While these strategies are effective and profit-increasing from the companies' perspective, they also raise ethical questions. The targeted manipulation of purchasing decisions can lead consumers to spend more than they can afford or to buy products they do not really need. Particularly vulnerable are groups such as adolescents or people with low self-esteem, who are more susceptible to such manipulative techniques.

Through these strategies, digital consumption has reached a new level in which the act of buying is no longer determined solely by the consumer's needs but is largely controlled by external stimuli. Understanding these mechanisms is essential for dealing more consciously with one's own purchasing decisions and critically questioning the influence of digital platforms.

In addition to scarcity, gamification itself is playing an increasingly important role in digital consumption. Reward systems, points, and discount promotions create a game-like experience that entices us to spend more time and money on a platform. A practical example shows how these mechanisms work: Tom, a 28-year-old graphic designer, reports how he was lured by a discount promotion on a shopping platform. "I actually just wanted to buy a pair of pants, but because of the 'buy three, pay for two' promotion, I ended up buying five items I didn't really need." The combination of discount, scarcity, and a playful approach led him to completely change his original purchasing plans.

> **Important**
>
> Digital platforms and social media deliberately exploit our weaknesses to control our buying behavior. Awareness of these mechanisms is the first step to escaping them and consuming more consciously.

However, the influence of advertising and social media does not end with the purchase. They also change our thinking about consumption. The constant confrontation with idealized images and messages creates the impression that a happy life is inextricably linked to the possession of certain products. This "materialism illusion" leads to consumption no longer being seen as a means to an end, but as an end in itself. Young people are particularly at risk, as their identities are still being formed and they are more dependent on social validation (Kasser, 2002).

> **Reference to Exercise 5**
>
> You will find this exercise in Sect. 9.3.5 "Consciously Questioning Buying Impulses." It offers you simple and practical strategies to manage your consumption behavior more consciously and to critically question buying impulses. Take the time to integrate this exercise into your daily life and observe how it changes your perception and decisions.

The challenge is to become aware of these influences and to develop strategies to counteract them. One possibility is to promote media literacy, which helps us to critically question advertising and digital content. It is equally important to practice mindfulness in dealing with social media and digital platforms, for example by taking conscious breaks or limiting screen time.

Summary

- **Psychological manipulation through advertising and social media:**
  Advertising and social media deliberately use psychological mechanisms such as emotional arousal, social comparison, and algorithmic personalization to generate buying impulses. These strategies tap deeply into needs for belonging, recognition, and happiness, thus steering our consumption behavior. Influencer marketing and gamification reinforce this effect by presenting consumption as part of an idealized lifestyle or playful experience.
- **Dynamics of digital consumption:**
  Personalized algorithms and techniques such as scarcity, social proof, and reward systems create a highly stimulating consumer experience that emotionally charges the act of buying and often bypasses rational thinking. These mechanisms aim to promote impulse purchases and increase attachment to digital platforms, which can be particularly problematic for vulnerable groups such as adolescents.
- **Societal and individual consequences:**
- The constant promotion of consumption by digital platforms changes our thinking and fosters a materialistic illusion in which personal happiness is closely linked to the possession of goods. This leads to financial pressure, environmental burdens, and social inequalities. To counteract these influences, media literacy, mindfulness, and critical questioning of digital content are key measures.

Advertising, social media, and digital consumption use targeted psychological strategies to influence our buying behavior and make us addicted. This section has shown how important it is to recognize these mechanisms in order to make autonomous decisions and escape manipulative influence.

4.3   How Society and Culture Shape Our Consumption Habits

Example

In this section, you will learn how cultural norms and societal dynamics influence our consumption habits and what role they play in the development of compulsive buying behavior.

Our consumption habits are directly rooted in the fundamental social structures of our society. They are not shaped solely by individual preferences or needs, but are the result of a complex interplay of cultural norms, social dynamics, and economic systems. In a world that presents consumption as a universal solution to life's problems, the act of purchasing is understood not only as a response to need, but as a means of self-definition, social positioning, and emotional coping. This section examines how societal and cultural factors foster and sustain compulsive consumption.

Cultural norms that glorify consumption as an expression of individuality and freedom play a central role. In Western societies, material possessions are often equated with success, self-fulfillment, and social recognition. These values are continuously reinforced and internalized through advertising, media, and entertainment. Advertising not only conveys the message that happiness and fulfillment are attainable through the purchase of certain products, but also suggests that abstaining from consumption is tantamount to personal failure. The consumer is pushed into a role where the acquisition of goods becomes the benchmark for personal happiness and social worth.

This cultural myth of a "better life through consumption" leads to the act of buying being not merely a functional action, but one imbued with deeper symbolic meaning. Purchasing a product becomes an act of self-presentation, communicating identity, values, and social belonging (Baudrillard, 1998). Thus, a consumer culture emerges in which goods are interpreted as cultural codes that mark social differences and signal belonging. A smartphone is purchased not only for its functionality, but also because it conveys a certain image of modernity and status. A designer handbag is not just a practical accessory, but a statement about style, class, and exclusivity.

This symbolism of consumption is particularly evident in cultural rituals that are increasingly shaped by purchasing behavior. Whether it's elaborate Christmas gifts, the luxurious wedding dress, or extravagant graduation parties—consumption is firmly embedded in rituals meant to strengthen community, tradition, and identity. However, these rituals are often accompanied by expectations and pressures that increase the drive to consume. Those who do not give generous gifts or host exceptional celebrations risk being perceived as less successful or committed. Thus, consumption becomes not only a means of self-presentation, but also an expression of social capital used in competition with others. The compulsion to consume is further amplified by social media, which provide a platform for the constant display of lifestyles and possessions. Platforms like Instagram, TikTok, or Pinterest set new standards for what is considered a "successful life." Here, the possession of luxury goods, expensive trips, or exclusive experiences becomes a prerequisite for social status and recognition. This phenomenon of the "cultural showcase" not only reinforces consumption patterns but also intensifies the sense of social comparison, which can lead to dissatisfaction and a heightened urge to buy (Belk, 2013). Another aspect of this cultural dynamic is the increasing short-lived nature of products, which can be described as a throwaway mentality. Fashion trends, technological innovations, and planned obsolescence create an environment in which consumer goods quickly lose value and must constantly be replaced by new purchases. This practice is not only ecologically problematic, but also reinforces the feeling that personal worth and social belonging depend on the up-to-dateness of one's possessions. The consumer is drawn into a cycle of buying, using, and replacing, leaving little room for reflection or sustainable choices. However, the cultural glorification of consumption also has psychological consequences. It can lead to a sense of inner emptiness, as the symbolic value of goods rarely provides the deeper fulfillment people actually seek. The attempt to define identity and status through consumption often creates a fragile self-perception dependent on external validation. Studies show that people who strongly pursue materialistic values are more likely to experience dissatisfaction, anxiety, and low self-esteem (Kasser, 2002). Thus, consumption becomes a substitute for genuine fulfillment and social connections—a mechanism that brings short-term satisfaction but can intensify feelings of alienation in the long run. The influence of social dynamics that increase consumption pressure is particularly strong. Comparing oneself to others—whether friends, colleagues, or celebrities—intensifies the need to keep up with societal standards. In a world shaped by social media, this comparison is almost unavoidable. Platforms like Instagram or TikTok provide a stage for self-presentation, where consumer goods are staged as symbols of success, beauty, or happiness. An example of this is the "unboxing culture," where influencers showcase their latest purchases and encourage their followers to buy similar products. This dynamic not only increases consumption pressure but also promotes the normalization of excessive buying behavior, which is portrayed as socially acceptable or even desirable (Belk, 2013).

Another example is the role of consumption in collective social norms. In many societies, the possession of certain goods is equated with social recognition and belonging. The decision to buy a new smartphone, a brand, or a car is determined not only by practical utility, but by the symbolic meaning the product conveys. The introduction of new technologies or fashion trends also creates the feeling of constantly needing to stay up to date. This dynamic leads to consumption compulsions being experienced not only individually, but collectively. Those who do not keep up risk being perceived as backward or "left out."

Cultural and societal factors not only shape individuals' consumption habits, but also create structures that promote and sustain excessive buying behavior. A particularly striking example is the increasingly popular "Buy now, pay later" model. This system facilitates consumption on credit by enabling the immediate acquisition of goods while deferring the financial burden to the future. The psychological barriers normally associated with spending money are thus effectively bypassed. The feeling that the actual financial cost will only become relevant later lowers the threshold for impulse purchases and encourages an attitude in which short-term gratification is prioritized over long-term financial security.

This mechanism is further reinforced by the prevailing culture of instant gratification, which is deeply rooted in many Western societies. This culture emphasizes quick results, immediate satisfaction of needs, and the avoidance of waiting. The ability to delay gratification—a central component of self-control and sustainable behavior—is increasingly devalued in such a context. Instead, the narrative is promoted that everything must be instantly available: from streaming services to fast deliveries to credit that enables the purchase of luxury goods. The linkage of economic systems with cultural values is crucial here. Economic mechanisms such as the "Buy now, pay later" model not only reflect existing values, but actively contribute to intensifying consumption compulsions. They create an environment in which consumption is promoted as a means of problem-solving and increasing personal happiness. This is supported by marketing strategies that specifically target emotional needs and present products as indispensable solutions to personal or social problems.

An example of this is the way advertising often creates a sense of urgency. Messages like "Only for a limited time" or "Last chance" use psychological mechanisms to create the impression that immediate action is required. These tactics reinforce impulsive buying behavior and help increase the willingness to use credit models like "Buy now, pay later." This demonstrates how economic and cultural factors intertwine to shape consumption patterns that are often adopted unconsciously.

In addition to advertising, social media also play a central role in promoting excessive consumption. Platforms like Instagram or TikTok not only create spaces for self-presentation, but also function as marketplaces where products can be directly advertised and purchased. The ability to buy products directly through a platform, combined with the presentation of idealized lifestyles, intensifies the social pressure to keep up with certain consumption patterns. This form of "social shopping" makes consumption not only more everyday, but also more subtle, as it is closely linked to the need for social belonging and recognition.

However, the structural conditions that promote excessive consumption go beyond the mechanisms of advertising and digital marketing. They are deeply embedded in economic and social systems. A materialistic society in which success and status are closely linked to possessions and consumption creates a cultural context that not only enables but actively rewards excessive buying behavior. This is evident in the social acceptance of debt, especially when it is incurred to acquire status symbols such as cars, expensive clothing, or electronic products. The possibility of fulfilling material desires through credit models is often not seen as problematic, but as a legitimate way to participate in a consumer-oriented society.

> **Important**
>
> Reflecting on the cultural and societal influences on one's own consumption behavior is crucial for making more conscious purchasing decisions. A critical look at social norms and media messages can help reduce pressure and clarify one's own values.

The interconnection of society and consumption has far-reaching consequences. Individuals become caught in a constant cycle of comparison, consumption, and dissatisfaction, while society as a whole fosters a culture of abundance that exacerbates ecological and social inequalities. The influence of cultural and social dynamics is subtle but omnipresent—from the way advertising addresses us to the expectations we place on ourselves and others.

> **Summary**
>
> - **Cultural and societal shaping of consumption behavior:** In many societies, consumption is portrayed as an expression of individuality, social status, and success. Advertising, social media, and cultural norms reinforce the symbolic meaning of goods and promote consumption patterns that are often based not on actual need, but on emotional and social desires.
> - **Mechanisms promoting consumption:** Economic strategies such as the "Buy now, pay later" model and the use of social media create an environment that facilitates impulsive buying behavior and increases consumption pressure. These mechanisms use psychological principles such as urgency or the need for social belonging to subtly influence consumption patterns.

- **Consequences and reflection:** Excessive consumption leads not only to individual problems such as dissatisfaction, financial burdens, and dependency, but also has societal and ecological impacts. Conscious reflection on cultural and societal influences is essential for clarifying personal values and breaking the cycle of comparison, consumption, and dissatisfaction.

This section has shown how cultural norms and societal dynamics shape our consumption habits and what role they play in the development of compulsive buying behavior. Reflecting on these influences is the first step toward separating one's own values and priorities from societal pressure and dealing more consciously with consumption incentives.

References

Baudrillard, J. (1998). *The consumer society: Myths and structures*. Sage.

Baumeister, R. F., & Leary, M. R. (1995). The need to belong: Desire for interpersonal attachments as a fundamental human motivation. *Psychological Bulletin, 117*(3), 497–529.

Belk, R. W. (2013). Extended self in a digital world. *Journal of Consumer Research, 40*(3), 477–500.

Bourdieu, P. (1984). *Distinction: A social critique of the judgement of taste*. Harvard University Press.

Chaplin, L. N., & John, D. R. (2007). Growing up in a material world: Age differences in materialism in children and adolescents. *Journal of Consumer Research, 34*(4), 480–493.

Dittmar, H. (2008). *Consumer culture, identity and well-being: the search for the "good life" and the "body perfect"*. Psychology Press.

Haws, K. L., & Poynor, C. (2008). Seize the Day! Encouraging Indulgence for the Here and Now. *Journal of Consumer Research, 35*(4), 680–691.

Hirschman, E. C. (1992). The consciousness of addiction: Toward a general theory of compulsive consumption. *Journal of Consumer Research, 19*(2), 155–179.

Kahneman, D., & Tversky, A. (1979). Prospect theory: An analysis of decision under risk. *Econometrica, 47*(2), 263–291.

Kasser, T. (2002). *The high price of materialism*. MIT Press.

McCracken, G. (1988). *Culture and consumption: New approaches to the symbolic Character of consumer goods and activities*. Indiana University Press.

Müller, S. (2021). *Die Psychologie des Kaufens: Warum wir Dinge wollen, die wir nicht brauchen*. München: Hanser.

Rook, D. W. (1987). The buying impulse. *Journal of Consumer Research, 14*(2), 189–199.

Tversky, A., & Kahneman, D. (1991). Loss aversion in riskless choice: A reference-dependent model. *The Quarterly Journal of Economics, 106*(4), 1039–1061.

Vohs, K. D., & Faber, R. J. (2007). Spent resources: Self-regulatory resource availability affects impulse buying. *Journal of Consumer Research, 33*(4), 537–547.
Zuboff, S. (2019). *The age of surveillance capitalism: The fight for a human future at the new frontier of power*. PublicAffairs.

5

The Way Out of the Consumption Trap

Abstract This chapter presents concrete strategies for controlling impulse purchases and sustainably changing one's own consumption behavior. Mindfulness is introduced as a key concept for making conscious purchasing decisions. Practical methods for self-control, such as deliberately delaying purchases or avoiding purchase triggers, are described. Another focus is on financial organization: those who structure their finances and develop a clear awareness of their expenses can gradually free themselves from the consumption spiral.

Overcoming consumer addiction requires more than insight—it demands targeted strategies, conscious decisions, and a new perspective on how we handle resources. Chapter 5 offers practical approaches to control impulse purchases, achieve financial stability, and develop a more sustainable lifestyle. With tools such as mindfulness, budget planning, and structured methods, this chapter demonstrates how you can gradually regain control over your consumption habits. It is an invitation not only to break old patterns, but also to create a positive, long-term change in your relationship with consumption and money.

O. Hoffmann, *Rethink Consumption*, https://doi.org/10.1007/978-3-662-72946-5_5

5.1 Mindfulness as a Key: How to Perceive Yourself and Your Needs

> **Example**
>
> In this section, you will learn how mindfulness can serve as an effective tool to better understand your feelings and buying impulses, and to approach your consumption behavior more consciously.

In a world characterized by constant sensory overload and consumer incentives, it is often difficult to clearly recognize one's own needs. Consumption is frequently used as a quick fix for emotional or social problems, without us being aware of the underlying feelings. Mindfulness offers a crucial approach here to break the dynamic between our emotions, thoughts, and actions. It enables us to pause, recognize our true needs, and thus make conscious decisions instead of acting impulsively.

The core of mindfulness lies in the ability to consciously perceive the present moment—without judgment, without distraction. This attitude creates space to reflect on buying impulses before they turn into action. Instead of immediately reacting to a perceived lack, mindful awareness offers the opportunity to pause and ask yourself: "Do I really need this? Or am I trying to compensate for another need right now?" This simple yet profound practice can help to sustainably reduce impulsive buying behavior (Kabat-Zinn, 2003).

However, mindfulness means more than just creating a moment to pause. It requires recognizing the underlying emotions and thoughts that often trigger automatic behaviors. In practice, this means not only paying attention to the buying impulse, but also to the feelings that precede it—be it stress, boredom, insecurity, or the need for social recognition. This conscious awareness makes it possible to take a step back and find alternatives for dealing with these emotions without resorting to consumption (Siegel, 2010). A central component of mindfulness practice is training the so-called "mindful pause." This technique teaches you to interrupt the automatic link between impulse and reaction. For example: when a buying impulse arises, you might consciously decide to wait at least five minutes before acting. During this time, you can observe your own thoughts and feelings without being overwhelmed by them. This brief interruption is often enough to let the impulse subside and make a more conscious decision (Shapiro et al., 2006).

Another benefit of mindfulness lies in fostering self-compassion. Many people who consume impulsively do so out of an inner sense of lack or inadequacy. Mindfulness helps to recognize these negative self-evaluations and replace them with self-compassion. Instead of comforting yourself by buying things, you can learn to regulate your emotions by meeting yourself with understanding and acceptance (Neff, 2011).

The effects of mindfulness practice, however, go beyond individual behavior. It helps to establish a deeper connection to one's own values and priorities. Many people report that through mindfulness, they develop a clearer understanding of what truly matters to them—be it time with family and friends, personal development, or sustainable lifestyles. This orientation helps shift the focus away from consumption as a supposed source of happiness and toward a more fulfilling way of life (Brown & Ryan, 2003).

> **Important**
>
> Mindfulness is not a short-term solution, but a long-term practice. Consciously perceiving your own impulses and needs requires patience and practice, but it offers the opportunity to change fundamental behavioral patterns and sustainably reduce impulsive consumption.

> **Note**
>
> Take another close look at Exercise 1 in this context.

An example illustrates the effectiveness of mindfulness in everyday life: Markus, a 41-year-old IT manager, noticed that after stressful meetings he often ended up in online shops and bought things he didn't really need. By mindfully observing his thoughts and feelings, he realized that his buying impulse was often triggered by a desire for control and relief. By starting to pause for a minute and take a deep breath before each purchase, he was able to interrupt many of these impulses. Instead of buying something, he often chose to take a short walk or allow himself a conscious break. This small change had a big impact on his consumption behavior and his emotional balance.

Mindfulness not only works on an individual level, but also changes how we perceive societal consumption patterns. It enables us to see through the subtle manipulations of advertising and social media and to distance ourselves from them. Those who are mindful recognize that many purchasing decisions are influenced less by real needs than by external stimuli. This realization strengthens personal autonomy and helps to break free from external expectations.

The practice of mindfulness can be integrated into everyday life through simple exercises. A particularly effective method is the conscious breathing exercise, in which you focus on your breath for a few minutes and try to observe every buying impulse without judgment. Afterwards, note your thoughts and feelings associated with the impulse. This reflection can help you recognize patterns and make more conscious decisions.

> **Practical Tip**
>
> Keep a "purchase journal" in which you not only record what you buy, but also why you bought it and how you felt about it. This simple tool can provide surprising insights and strengthen your mindfulness in dealing with consumption in the long term.

Mindfulness does not mean giving up consumption entirely, but rather making more conscious decisions about what truly matters. It allows you to put your own values and needs at the forefront, instead of overshadowing them with impulsive actions. This process can not only change buying behavior, but also improve quality of life. Those who consume mindfully do not invest in things they do not need, but in what truly enriches them—be it time, relationships, or personal development.

> **Summary**
>
> - **Understanding and reflecting on consumer addiction:** Mindfulness helps to recognize the underlying emotional and cognitive mechanisms of consumption behavior. It enables you to question impulsive purchasing decisions by making the moment between impulse and action conscious. Through exercises such as pausing before a purchase or observing your own thoughts, automated behavioral patterns can be broken.
> - **Making conscious decisions:** Mindfulness strengthens the ability to distinguish real needs from short-term desires. Techniques such as breathing exercises or keeping a purchase journal can help establish more conscious consumption habits. This creates space to make decisions in line with your own values, rather than being guided by external stimuli and societal pressure.
> - **Long-term change and quality of life:** Through the continuous practice of mindfulness, not only is consumption behavior changed, but emotional

resilience is also strengthened. Mindfulness fosters self-compassion, a deeper understanding of one's own needs, and increased life satisfaction. Those who consume consciously invest in what truly enriches them—be it personal development, relationships, or sustainable values.

Mindfulness is a powerful tool for breaking impulsive buying behavior and better understanding your own needs. This section has shown how mindful practice can help you approach consumption more consciously and how this attitude can sustainably improve your quality of life.

5.2   Strategies for Controlling Impulse Purchases

Example

In this section, you will learn how to recognize impulsive buying behavior and control it with effective strategies in order to make more conscious and sustainable decisions.

Impulse purchases are a central feature of problematic consumption behavior and are often the result of emotional or social triggers. They usually occur spontaneously, without thorough consideration or weighing of the consequences. While the act of buying often brings a feeling of joy or control, it is frequently followed by disappointment, guilt, or stress—especially when the financial means for the purchase are lacking. To break this cycle, it is necessary to understand the mechanisms behind impulsive consumption behavior and to develop targeted strategies that make this behavior manageable.

One of the most effective measures against impulse purchases is creating awareness. Impulse purchases are often unconscious reactions to external stimuli such as special offers, advertising, or social media. Studies show that many people buy impulsively to feel better in the short term or to relieve stress (Rook, 1987). By consciously reflecting on your own buying motives, these patterns can be recognized and interrupted. A helpful question, for example, is: "Do I really need this product, or am I trying to solve another problem?" The answer to this question often creates the necessary distance to question impulsive behavior. Additionally, keeping a "purchase diary" can help you get to the bottom of your own buying habits. By regularly noting what you bought, why you bought it, and how you felt about it, your buying behavior becomes more transparent. Such a diary can reveal patterns that were previously unconscious, such as buying out of boredom or repeatedly responding to certain marketing strategies. Keeping a purchase diary also makes it possible to identify specific situations in which impulse purchases occur particularly frequently, and to develop targeted strategies to address them. Another approach is to create obstacles in the purchasing process. This can be achieved through simple but effective measures such as deleting saved payment information in online shops or avoiding credit card payments. Studies show that the need to actively enter payment data significantly reduces the likelihood of impulsive decisions (Baumeister et al., 2007). Furthermore, a so-called "waiting period rule" can be introduced: before buying a non-essential product, wait 24 hours and check whether the desire for the product still exists. Often, the initial urge fades once the emotional motivation subsides.

Mindfulness practices have also proven effective in reducing impulsive buying behavior. Techniques such as breathing exercises or consciously perceiving emotions can help you consciously experience the moment of the buying impulse without immediately giving in to it. Mindfulness fosters an inner distance from impulsive decisions and enables you to recognize them as temporary reactions that do not necessarily have to result in action (Shapiro et al., 2006). Regular mindfulness practice can help to sustainably change behavior in the long term.

In addition to personal reflection and conscious decision-making, the design of your environment also plays a crucial role. Unsubscribing from newsletters or blocking advertisements on social media platforms can reduce the number of purchase incentives. It is also helpful to use a shopping list with clearly defined products when shopping to avoid spontaneous purchases. These external changes support conscious control over the purchasing process and reduce the likelihood of falling back into impulsive patterns.

Another key to controlling impulse purchases lies in delaying them. The so-called "30-second, 24-hour, or 30-day trick" has proven effective in many cases. Here, the person commits to pausing briefly before each purchase and considering whether the purchase is really necessary. For larger purchases, a longer reflection period of several days or weeks may be appropriate. This delay gives the brain the opportunity to process the emotional component of the desire to buy and promotes more rational decision-making (Baumeister, 2002).

> **Note on Exercise 6**
>
> To specifically control impulsive buying behavior, you will find in Sect. 9.3.6 the "Interrupting Impulses Strategy," a structured method that helps you recognize buying impulses, consciously question them, and replace them with alternative coping strategies. This exercise supports you in making more sustainable decisions and reflecting on your relationship with consumption.

A practical example illustrates this strategy: Markus, a 40-year-old marketing expert, notices that he often buys expensive electronic devices without really needing them. By applying the 30-day rule, he found that most of his buying impulses faded after a few days. He was not only able to save money, but also develop stronger self-control. This experience helped him to redefine his relationship with consumption.

Minimizing consumption incentives is another effective strategy. Many impulse purchases occur because products are too easily accessible—whether through online shopping, credit cards, or aggressive advertising strategies. Consciously removing consumption stimuli can therefore help reduce impulsive behavior. This could mean unsubscribing from online shop newsletters, using credit cards only for planned purchases, or installing ad blockers on digital devices. Such simple measures create an environment that is less conducive to making unconsidered decisions (Faber & Vohs, 2010).

Developing a clear budget and a shopping list are also effective tools. By planning in advance what is to be purchased, the temptation to make unforeseen purchases is significantly reduced. At the same time, budgeting encourages a conscious engagement with your own financial resources and priorities. This method is particularly effective when combined with regular reflection on your own spending, such as by keeping an expense journal.

> **Practical Tip**
>
> Start with small, actionable steps. For example, apply the 30-second rule on your next shopping trip or review which newsletters you really need. Small changes can have a big impact in the long run.

In addition to these concrete strategies, it is crucial to analyze the emotional triggers for impulse purchases in more detail, as they are often the driving force behind uncontrolled consumption behavior. Negative emotions such as stress, frustration, loneliness, or even boredom frequently act as triggers that prompt people to seek short-term gratification through consumption. These emotional states activate the need for a quick solution, and the act of buying appears to be an easy and immediately effective way out.

To break this cycle, it is helpful to develop alternative coping strategies that not only address the underlying emotional needs but also contribute to better well-being in the long term. Mindfulness exercises such as meditation or breathing techniques can, for example, help you consciously perceive and regulate your emotional state instead of reacting impulsively. Studies have shown that regular mindfulness practice not only reduces stress but also strengthens the ability to control impulses and make conscious decisions (Kabat-Zinn, 2003).

In addition to mindfulness practices, physical activities such as jogging, yoga, or dancing can serve as effective alternatives. Exercise releases endorphins, which, like the act of buying, create a feeling of satisfaction and reward, but without the negative consequences of consumption. At the same time, physical activity promotes self-esteem and strengthens resilience to external stressors.

Creative activities such as painting, writing, or making music also offer a valuable way to relieve emotional tension and cultivate positive feelings. Creative processes not only promote concentration and self-reflection, but also create a space in which people can engage with their emotions on a deeper level. For many affected individuals, these activities represent a sustainable form of self-care that contributes to a more balanced lifestyle in the long term.

Another important approach is to foster social interactions. Loneliness is a common trigger for impulsive consumption behavior, as the act of buying can temporarily mask feelings of emptiness and isolation. Building and maintaining social relationships—whether through shared activities, conversations, or joining interest groups—can fill this emotional void in a healthy way. Social contacts not only provide support and recognition, but also have a stabilizing effect on emotional balance.

Practical Tip

Create a list of activities that bring you joy and also help you cope with negative emotions. Use this list as a resource the next time you feel the urge to buy impulsively. Experiment with different strategies to find out what works best for you.

These alternative strategies are not only effective in preventing impulse purchases, but also promote a conscious and reflective lifestyle. They help shift the focus from short-term gratification to long-term satisfaction and emotional stability. By recognizing emotional triggers and developing alternative solutions, people can regain control over their consumption behavior and sustainably improve their quality of life at the same time.

Important

Strategies for controlling impulse purchases require patience and consistency. Not every approach works equally well for everyone. It is worthwhile to try out different methods and adapt them individually.

Summary

- **Create awareness and promote reflection:** Impulse purchases are often based on unconscious reactions to external stimuli such as advertising or stress. Consciously reflecting on your own buying motives, for example by asking "Do I really need this product?" or keeping a purchase diary, helps to recognize patterns and question impulsive behavior.
- **Use purchase barriers and mindfulness:** Strategies such as the "waiting period rule" (e.g., waiting 24 hours before buying), deleting saved payment data, or unsubscribing from newsletters create distance from impulse purchases. In addition, mindfulness practices such as meditation or breathing exercises can help to consciously perceive emotional triggers and regain control over spontaneous buying impulses.
- **Develop alternative coping strategies:** Emotional triggers such as stress or loneliness can be sustainably managed through activities like sports, creative pursuits, or building social contacts. These alternatives promote well-being, strengthen self-control, and shift the focus from short-term gratification to long-term emotional stability.

This section has shown that impulse purchases are not an inevitable behavior, but can be controlled with conscious strategies. By combining reflection, planning, and reducing consumption incentives, you can reduce impulsive buying behavior and develop a more conscious, sustainable approach to consumption. The first step is to observe yourself and understand the mechanisms behind your purchasing decisions.

5.3 Creating Financial Order: Regaining Control

> **Example**
>
> In this section, you will learn how to reorganize your finances to gain control and stability. The focus is on establishing the foundations for a mindful approach to money and achieving long-term financial security.

Financial disorder is not only a consequence of compulsive buying, but often also an aggravating factor. Those who lose track of their finances often find themselves in a vicious cycle of impulse purchases, growing debt, and a sense of loss of control. Restoring financial order is therefore a central step toward achieving sustainable changes in money management and consumption. It is not just a matter of numbers, but also of the attitudes and habits that shape our financial reality.

A first step toward financial order is complete transparency regarding income and expenses. Many people underestimate how much they actually spend, especially on small, recurring items such as coffee, snacks, or online subscriptions. These so-called "invisible expenses" quickly add up, causing budgets to be exceeded and a sense of loss of control to arise. Tracking all financial transactions—whether through an app, a household ledger, or a simple Excel spreadsheet—provides clarity about actual financial priorities and enables targeted changes to be made.

A practical example: Sarah, a 29-year-old graphic designer, discovered through analyzing her bank statements that she was spending over €150 a month on small online orders—a sum that added up to a significant amount over the year. She also found that several subscriptions she hardly used were further straining her budget. By consciously examining such expenses, Sarah began to systematically question her purchases and distinguish between necessary and impulsive spending. She set clear financial goals and not only reduced her expenses, but also experienced a strengthened sense of self-control.

In addition to analyzing existing expenses, it is equally important to identify individual triggers for impulsive buying behavior. Often, emotional states such as boredom, stress, or the need for reward lead to unconsidered purchases. Here, targeted emotion regulation strategies, such as mindfulness exercises or alternative activities, can help break these patterns. For example, Sarah discovered that she often shopped out of boredom. Instead of buying immediately, she implemented a 24-hour rule: purchases that were not urgently needed were put on hold, and she checked the next day whether the desire still existed. This simple technique helped her significantly reduce her spending.

Another crucial step is setting a realistic budget that takes into account both fixed and variable costs. A budget not only serves as a means of control, but also provides the freedom to consciously spend money on things that truly matter. For example, Sarah used her newfound financial awareness to allocate a monthly amount for spontaneous but considered purchases. This gave her the feeling of still being able to treat herself without jeopardizing her overarching goals. It is also advisable to set aside reserves for unexpected expenses or major purchases. People are often thrown off course financially by sudden costs, such as car repairs or medical bills. An emergency fund amounting to three to six months' salary can help manage such situations without additional strain. Sarah started with small amounts, which she transferred monthly to a separate account. Building this safety net gave her not only stability but also an increased sense of independence.

Consciously engaging with income and expenses is not only a means to financial order, but also a path to a more self-determined life. Transparency and planning provide the foundation for making financial decisions proactively rather than reactively. The goal is not to restrict consumption entirely, but to make it more mindful and purposeful. Sarah's example shows how gradual change can not only improve the financial situation, but also enhance personal well-being and quality of life.

In addition to transparency, prioritizing expenses is also crucial. Financial order does not mean giving up everything, but making conscious decisions about which expenses truly matter. A proven tool for this is the so-called "50/30/20 model," in which 50% of income is allocated to basic needs (rent, food), 30% to personal wants, and 20% to savings or debt repayment (Harvard Business Review, 2019). This model provides a clear structure and allows financial stability to be combined with a certain degree of flexibility (Warren & Tyagi, 2005).

Note on Exercise 7

This exercise offers a structured way to analyze your financial situation and establish new behaviors. It is especially valuable for individuals who want to break free from impulsive consumption and achieve long-term stability. You will find the detailed description in Section 9.3.7 "Financial Reflection and Goal

> Setting." Use the steps to gain clarity, identify triggers, and consciously set new financial priorities.

Another key aspect is dealing with debt. Many people suffering from compulsive buying carry a heavy financial burden from credit card debt, consumer loans, or other liabilities. These debts not only increase financial stress, but also affect emotional well-being by triggering feelings of guilt, shame, and loss of control. Escaping the debt trap therefore requires not only financial planning, but also psychological support and long-term behavioral change.

Debt repayment should be systematic and strategic in order to reduce psychological pressure and regain a sense of control. A particularly popular and effective method is the so-called "snowball method." Here, the smallest debts are paid off first, while minimum payments continue to be made on larger liabilities (Ramsey, 2011). Once a debt is fully paid off, the freed-up amount is applied to the next largest debt. This process continues until all debts are repaid. The snowball method has two key advantages: on the one hand, it allows for quick wins that boost motivation. On the other hand, it gives those affected a growing sense of self-efficacy, which helps overcome negative emotions such as shame or hopelessness. Another proven concept is the so-called "avalanche method." In contrast to the snowball method, this strategy focuses on debts with the highest interest rates in order to minimize interest costs in the long term. This method is particularly effective for people whose debts are growing rapidly due to high interest rates. However, it requires a high degree of discipline, as visible progress is often slower, which can be challenging for emotionally burdened debtors (Amar et al., 2011). The psychological component should not be underestimated either. Studies show that debt is closely linked to psychological burdens such as anxiety, depression, and low self-esteem (Richardson et al., 2013). Mindful handling of these emotions is essential to prevent feelings of guilt from leading to renewed consumption behavior. Support services such as debt counseling or therapeutic approaches focused on financial stress management can help reduce emotional strain and at the same time promote sustainable behavioral change. In addition, technological tools can play an important role. Financial planning apps such as "Mint" or "YNAB" (You Need A Budget) offer practical tools for monitoring expenses, sticking to budgets, and creating debt repayment plans. These digital solutions are especially helpful for people who have difficulty organizing their finances manually, and they enable transparent and regular monitoring of progress.

Ultimately, dealing with debt is not just a matter of financial planning, but also of personal attitude. The goal should not only be to pay off debt, but also to change the way one handles money and consumption. Long-term success requires that those affected learn to make financial decisions more consciously, assess their needs more realistically, and question consumption as an emotional coping mechanism.

However, financial order does not only mean reducing debt and controlling expenses, but also building up reserves. An emergency fund covering three to six months of expenses provides security and reduces dependence on short-term loans. Studies show that people with financial reserves are less susceptible to stress and make impulsive consumption decisions less frequently (Hsee & Rottenstreich, 2004). A solid financial cushion is therefore not only practical, but also strengthens emotional resilience.

> **Practical Tip**
>
> Use digital tools or simple spreadsheets to organize your finances. Regular reviews, for example at the end of each week, help you stay on top of things and make adjustments before problems arise.

In addition to the practical reorganization of finances, developing a new mindset is also crucial. Financial order is based on a conscious attitude toward money. Money is not just a means of consumption, but a tool for achieving freedom and security. Reflecting on values and goals helps align spending with personal priorities and develop sustainable behavior in the long term.

> **In Summary**
>
> - **Transparency and analysis as a foundation:**
>   Restoring financial order begins with comprehensive transparency regarding income and expenses. Becoming aware of "invisible" expenses, such as recurring small amounts, enables targeted analysis and forms the basis for conscious decisions. Financial tools and budgeting models such as the "50/30/20 principle" provide practical guidance for effective financial planning.
> - **Debt management and emotional resilience:**
>   A systematic approach, such as the snowball or avalanche method, supports debt reduction and fosters a sense of control and self-efficacy. At the same time, it is essential to address psychological burdens such as guilt and anxiety to prevent relapses into impulsive consumption. Support through

counseling or therapeutic approaches can sustainably strengthen this process.

- **Long-term stability and new ways of thinking:**
  Financial order goes beyond debt reduction and includes building up reserves as well as developing a reflective approach to money. An emergency fund provides security, while a more mindful mindset helps align financial decisions with personal values and long-term goals. In this way, financial freedom is promoted as a sustainable life strategy.

Restoring financial order is a central step in overcoming compulsive buying and achieving financial stability. Transparency, prioritization, and the development of a new mindset are crucial for gaining long-term security and control. This section has shown that financial order is more than just numbers—it is an expression of conscious decisions and a clear life strategy.

References

Amar, M., Ariely, D., Ayal, S., Cryder, C. E., & Rick, S. I. (2011).Winning the battle but losing the war: The psychology of debt management. *Journal of Marketing Research, 48*(SPL), S. 38–S50.

Baumeister, R. F. (2002). *Losing control: how and why people fail at self-regulation.* Academic.

Baumeister, R. F., Vohs, K. D., & Tice, D. M. (2007). The strength model of self-control. *Current Dctions in Psychological Science, 16*(6), 351–355.

Brown, K. W., & Ryan, R. M. (2003). The benefits of being present: Mindfulness and its role in psychological well-being. *Journal of Personality and Social Psychology, 84*(4), 822–848.

Faber, R. J., & Vohs, K. D. (2010). Self-regulation and impulsive buying. *Perspectives on Psychological Science, 5*(3), 217–232.

Harvard Business Review. (2019). *The 50/30/20 rule of budgeting: A guide to financial success.* HBR.

Hsee, C. K., & Rottenstreich, Y. (2004). Music, pandas, and muggers: On the affective psychology of value. *Journal of Experimental Psychology: General, 133*(1), 23–30.

Kabat-Zinn, J. (2003). *Full catastrophe living: Using the wisdom of your body and mind to face stress, pain, and illness.* Bantam.

Neff, K. D. (2011). *Self-compassion: The proven power of being kind to yourself.* William Morrow.

Ramsey, D. (2011). *The total money makeover: A proven plan for financial fitness.* Thomas Nelson.

Richardson, T., Elliott, P., & Roberts, R. (2013). The Relationship between personal unsecured debt and mental and physical health: A systematic review and meta-analysis. *Clinical Psychology Review, 33*(8), 1148–1162.

Rook, D. W. (1987). The buying impulse. *Journal of Consumer Research, 14*(2), 189–199.

Shapiro, S. L., Carlson, L. E., Astin, J. A., & Freedman, B. (2006). Mechanisms of mindfulness. *Journal of Clinical Psychology, 62*(3), 373–386.

Siegel, D. J. (2010). *The mindful therapist: A clinician's guide to mindsight and neural integration.* W. W. Norton & Company.

Warren, E., & Tyagi, A. W. (2005). *All your worth: The ultimate lifetime money plan.* Free Press.

Further Reading

Ariely, D. (2008). *Predictably irrational: The hidden forces that shape our decisions.* Harper.

Baer, R. A. (2006). *Mindfulness-based treatment approaches: Clinician's guide to evidence base and applications.* Academic.

Dittmar, H. (2008). *Consumer culture, identity and well-being: The search for the „good life" and the „body perfect".* Psychology Press.

Fromm, E. (1976). *Haben oder Sein: Die seelischen Grundlagen einer neuen Gesellschaft.* Dtv.

Kahneman, D. (2011). *Thinking, fast and slow.* Farrar, Straus and Giroux.

Soman, D. (2001). Effects of payment mechanism on spending behavior: The role of rehearsal and immediacy of payments. *Journal of Consumer Research, 27*(4), 460–474.

Thaler, R. H., & Sunstein, C. R. (2008). *Nudge: Improving decisions about health, wealth, and happiness.* Yale University Press.

6

Discovering New Lifestyles

Abstract This paper presents alternative lifestyles that can lead to a more conscious approach to consumption. Minimalism is explained as a concept that not only contributes to the reduction of material possessions, but also provides psychological relief. Sustainable consumption is discussed as a counter-model to the throwaway society—particularly with regard to ecological and social responsibility. In addition, a balanced relationship between "having" and "being" is sought, in which consumption is not seen as an end in itself, but as a conscious decision in harmony with one's own values.

Our relationship with consumption shapes not only our daily lives, but also our identity and well-being. Chap. 6 invites you to gain new perspectives on your lifestyle and to discover alternatives to materialistic pursuits. It explores how minimalism, sustainable consumption, and a conscious engagement with "having" and "being" can contribute to a more balanced and fulfilling life. This chapter outlines ways to free yourself from unnecessary burdens and enhance your quality of life through mindful choices—for yourself and for the environment.

O. Hoffmann, *Rethink Consumption*, https://doi.org/10.1007/978-3-662-72946-5_6

6.1   Minimalism: Less Possession, More Life

> **Example**
>
> In this section, you will learn how minimalism as a conscious way of life can help improve your quality of life by focusing on what is essential and freeing yourself from unnecessary burdens.

Minimalism is more than an aesthetic movement or a passing trend—it is a philosophy that can have profound effects on personal well-being and lifestyle. In a society characterized by abundance and materialism, minimalism offers an alternative perspective: the conscious decision to part with unnecessary possessions and instead focus on the things that truly matter. This way of life stands in contrast to the widespread assumption that more possessions automatically bring more satisfaction.

The core idea of minimalism lies in the question of what is essential: What do I really need to lead a fulfilling life? Many people only realize how burdensome material possessions can be when they begin to critically question them. Too many possessions often lead to stress, financial strain, and a sense of being overwhelmed. At the same time, they distract from what is truly important—relationships, experiences, and personal values. Minimalism offers the opportunity to reprioritize and break free from the illusion that happiness can be bought (Kasser, 2002).

An example illustrates the transformative power of minimalism: Anna, a 42-year-old architect, decided after years of excessive consumption to simplify her life. She began systematically reducing her belongings and found that not only did she not use many things, but they also represented emotional baggage. "It was liberating to part with things that burdened me more than they enriched me," she says. After this process, she not only felt lighter but also gained more clarity about what truly matters to her in life: time with her family, creative projects, and personal growth.

The psychological benefits of minimalism are well documented. Studies show that reducing possessions can increase well-being by lowering stress and creating space for mindfulness (Carter & Gilovich, 2012). A minimalist lifestyle also fosters a sense of autonomy and self-determination, as the decision to own less is made actively and consciously. At the same time, minimalism supports sustainable ways of living by focusing on quality over quantity and reducing the environmental impact of consumption (Schmidt, 2021).

But minimalism is not just a matter of physical possessions. It is also about relieving mental and emotional resources. The flood of information, social media, and constant availability also contribute to many people feeling overwhelmed. A minimalist approach to digital life—such as reducing screen time or consciously selecting digital content—can be just as liberating as decluttering physical space (Newport, 2019).

Practical Tip

Start with small steps. Choose one area of your life—such as your wardrobe or your desk—and consider which items truly bring you joy or utility. Everything else can be let go. Repeat this process until you have found a clear structure and order.

However, minimalism is not a universal concept that looks the same for everyone. For some, it means living with as little as possible, while for others it simply means consuming more mindfully. What matters is that minimalism is used as a tool for self-reflection to create a life that aligns with individual values and needs. It is a way to make room for what truly counts—not through deprivation, but through conscious choices.

In Summary

- **Minimalism as a Life Philosophy:** Minimalism is more than reducing possessions—it is a conscious decision to focus on what is essential in life. This includes not only decluttering physical objects but also letting go of mental and emotional overload to gain clarity and satisfaction.
- **Psychological and Social Benefits:** Reducing possessions and consumption creates space for mindfulness, reduces stress, and fosters a sense of autonomy and self-determination. At the same time, minimalism shifts the focus to meaningful relationships, experiences, and personal values that contribute to greater quality of life in the long term.
- **Sustainability and Individual Adaptation:** Minimalism supports sustainable lifestyles by questioning consumption habits and minimizing the impact on the environment and society. Minimalism is individually adaptable—from extremely reduced lifestyles to more mindful consumption—and can be tailored to personal needs and values.

Minimalism is much more than decluttering your household—it is a way of life that can enhance personal well-being while also promoting social and ecological responsibility. By focusing on what is essential, we gain clarity, satisfaction, and freedom. Minimalism is an invitation to live more consciously and to let go of what does not enrich us.

6.2   Sustainable Consumption: How Mindful Shopping Can Make You Happy

Example

In this section, you will learn how a resource-conserving and mindful approach to consumer goods can not only protect the environment but also enhance your personal well-being.

In a world marked by abundance and waste, the idea of sustainable consumption may at first seem like a restriction. But the opposite is true: a mindful and resource-conserving approach to consumer goods opens up the possibility of reshaping our relationship with possessions and consumption, thereby achieving a deeper sense of satisfaction. Sustainability is not just an ecological concept, but also a way to slow down your lifestyle and focus on what is essential.

Sustainable consumption is based on the idea of using resources consciously and responsibly. This means buying less, but more intentionally, and considering a product's entire life cycle—from production to disposal. Studies show that people who choose sustainable consumption often experience an increased sense of self-efficacy (Kasser, 2002). The conscious renunciation of unnecessary consumption is not perceived as a limitation, but as liberation from the compulsion to constantly buy. This behavior not only benefits the environment but also creates space for a greater appreciation of the things we own.

A practical example illustrates this effect: Sarah, a 35-year-old teacher, decided two years ago to radically reduce her consumption and only buy products that were sustainably produced. At first, she felt overwhelmed by the limited choices, but over time she noticed how her decisions positively changed her life. "I learned to appreciate things I used to take for granted," she reports. Today, Sarah not only feels happier but also more connected to the values that matter to her, such as environmental protection and social justice.

The psychology of happiness shows that mindful consumption is not only more sustainable but also more fulfilling. Purchasing high-quality and durable products that align with one's own values leads to deeper satisfaction than acquiring short-lived consumer goods. In addition, sustainable shopping reduces the stress caused by impulsive buying or the pursuit of ever more possessions (Solomon, 2020). Instead, it fosters a sense of control and self-confidence, as the focus is on quality and ethical responsibility.

Another aspect of sustainable consumption is **community building**. People who shop mindfully often engage in networks such as swap meets, repair cafés, or local sustainability initiatives. These social interactions not only create a sense of belonging but also provide opportunities to learn from others and take responsibility together. Sustainable consumption thus becomes both a social and personal gain.

Practical Tip

Start with small steps, such as buying secondhand products or consciously choosing certified goods. Every step toward sustainability counts and can have a positive impact on your well-being and the environment.

The benefits of a resource-conserving approach to consumer goods go far beyond environmental protection. They also affect personal satisfaction, social relationships, and the feeling of contributing to something greater. By embracing sustainable consumption, we gain the opportunity to redefine the meaning of ownership and free ourselves from the constraints of materialistic thinking.

In Summary

- **Sustainable consumption promotes personal well-being and satisfaction:** The conscious renunciation of unnecessary consumption is experienced as liberation from the compulsion to constantly buy. Studies show that focusing on durable, high-quality products and ethical values can increase the sense of self-efficacy and life satisfaction.
- **Community and social interaction through sustainability:** Participation in networks such as swap meets or sustainability initiatives strengthens social bonds and creates a sense of belonging. Sustainable consumption thus becomes a communal experience and connects people through shared values.
- **Appreciation and responsibility for the environment and society:** Through resource-conserving behavior, people can not only protect the environment but also redefine their perspective on ownership and consumption. This fosters a deeper appreciation for the things they own and a stronger awareness of their responsibility toward society and future generations.

Sustainable consumption is much more than an ecological necessity—it is a key to a more mindful, happier life. By focusing on quality, values, and community, it opens up new ways to increase personal satisfaction while also making the world a little better.

6.3   The Path to a Balanced Relationship Between Having and Being

In this section, you will learn how to find a healthy balance between material needs and inner fulfillment by reflecting on your values and living more consciously.

The contrast between "having" and "being" is one of the central questions of modern societies. While "having" focuses on possessions, consumption, and external security, "being" stands for inner values such as contentment, mindfulness, and authentic relationships. Both aspects are essential for human well-being, but the balance between them often becomes skewed. In a consumer society that glorifies material possessions, "being" is often neglected in favor of "having." This section addresses the question of how we can establish a personal balance between these two poles in order to lead a more fulfilling life.

The overemphasis on "having" is evident in many areas of modern life. Material possessions are often equated with success and happiness, which leads people to define their identity and self-worth through their belongings. However, studies show that focusing on material wealth not only fails to bring lasting satisfaction but is even correlated with lower levels of well-being (Kasser, 2002). The reason is that the pursuit of possessions is often based on external expectations and has little to do with people's inner needs. Instead, a kind of "hedonic treadmill" arises, where the joy of new goods quickly fades and is replaced by the desire for more (Frederick & Loewenstein, 1999).

A practical example shows how a realignment toward a more balanced relationship between "having" and "being" can succeed. Michael, a successful entrepreneur, spent years striving to achieve more—a bigger house, more expensive cars, more luxurious vacations. Yet despite his financial success, he felt empty and unfulfilled. In a moment of reflection, he asked himself what truly made him happy. He began to invest less time and energy in acquiring goods and instead focused on personal relationships, creative hobbies, and his physical health. Michael realized that true fulfillment does not come from owning material things, but from the way he shapes his life.

The transition to a more conscious life requires a critical examination of one's own values. What role do possessions and consumption play in your life? To what extent do you define your worth by what you own? These questions can help direct your focus to what is truly important. Mindfulness is a crucial tool in this process. It enables you to experience moments consciously and to detach from external expectations. By focusing on "being"—through deeper social relationships, personal development, or the appreciation of simple pleasures—we create a foundation for long-term satisfaction.

Practical Tip

A simple exercise can be to keep a consumption diary. Note why you buy something and how you feel about it. Then reflect on whether the purchase actually contributed to your well-being or was meant to compensate for another need.

It is important to note, however, that "having" and "being" are not opposites but can complement each other. Material goods have their place and significance as long as they do not become the sole measure of life. A certain degree of possession provides security and allows you to focus on other aspects of life. The problem only arises when "having" dominates and "being" is pushed aside. The goal is to bring both aspects into a balance that suits individual needs.

Important

The balance between "having" and "being" is not a fixed quantity, but a dynamic process that changes over the course of life. It requires regular reflection and adjustment to remain in harmony with your own values and priorities.

Reference to Exercise 8

Throughout this section, the importance of consciously engaging with consumption habits and immaterial values is emphasized. To better understand your personal patterns and motives, it is recommended to complete Exercise 8 in Sect. 9.3.8 "The Consumption and Values Diary." You will find detailed instructions at the end of this section. This exercise will help you approach your needs more reflectively and develop a more sustainable, fulfilling lifestyle.

The search for this balance is not a quick process, but an ongoing development. It begins with the realization that the pursuit of possessions does not automatically lead to a fulfilling life, and with the willingness to explore new paths. By integrating mindfulness, reflection, and the appreciation of immaterial aspects, we can create a life that is enriched both internally and externally.

In Summary

- **The Imbalance Between "Having" and "Being":** In modern consumer societies, material possessions are often overvalued and equated with success and happiness, while inner values such as mindfulness, relationships, and contentment are neglected. This imbalance often leads to lower well-being and the illusion that happiness can be achieved through possessions.
- **Reflection and Mindfulness as Keys:** Consciously engaging with your own values and needs can help bring the relationship between "having" and "being" into balance. Practices such as mindfulness and focusing on personal relationships or immaterial joys foster long-term fulfillment and satisfaction.
- **Balance as a Dynamic Process:** The right balance between "having" and "being" is individual and changes over the course of life. Regular reflection and adjustment of priorities are necessary to remain true to your own values and to create a life that is enriched both materially and internally.

This section has shown how the balance between "having" and "being" can be achieved through reflection, mindfulness, and a realignment of values. A conscious approach to material needs and a focus on inner fulfillment are the keys to a balanced and fulfilling life.

References

Carter, T. J., & Gilovich, T. (2012). The relative relativity of material and experiential purchases. *Journal of Personality and Social Psychology, 102*(6), 1304–1315.

Frederick, S., & Loewenstein, G. (1999). *Hedonic adaptation. Well-being: The foundations of hedonic psychology.*

Kasser, T. (2002). *The high price of materialism.* MIT Press.

Newport, C. (2019). *Digital minimalism: Choosing a focused life in a noisy world.* Portfolio.

Schmidt, L. (2021). *Neuropsychologie des Konsums: Wie unser Gehirn den Markt formt.* Beltz.

Solomon, M. R. (2020). *Consumer behavior: Buying, having, and being.* Pearson.

7

Long-Term Change

Abstract This chapter addresses the sustainability of learned consumption strategies. Change requires not only short-term control over impulse purchases, but also long-term adjustments to one's own patterns of thinking. It explains how relapses can be recognized and managed, and how it is possible to build a life beyond consumer addiction. Psychological mechanisms of behavioral change, such as the importance of routines and positive reinforcement, are discussed.

Chapter 7 is dedicated to the question of how sustainable changes in dealing with consumer behavior can be achieved. The way out of the consumption trap is not a short-term process, but requires patience, reflection, and conscious decisions. But how can new habits be consolidated, and how should setbacks be handled? This chapter shows how you can shape a self-determined life beyond consumer addiction in the long term. It offers strategies to overcome old patterns and provides practical guidance for building a life based on your values and goals—free from compulsions and characterized by conscious being.

O. Hoffmann, *Rethink Consumption*, https://doi.org/10.1007/978-3-662-72946-5_7

7.1 How to Change Your Consumer Behavior Sustainably

Example

In this section, you will learn how to implement concrete steps to change your consumer behavior and consolidate them in the long term, in order to achieve a more conscious and sustainable lifestyle.

Changing consumption habits is a challenge that requires not only discipline but also a deep understanding of one's own motivations and patterns. Many people start out enthusiastically trying to change their consumption habits, but the long-term integration of new behaviors often fails. The reasons for this are often unrealistic expectations, lack of mindfulness, or a return to old routines triggered by external stimuli. This section addresses how you can achieve sustainable changes in your consumer behavior—not as a short-term measure, but as a deeply rooted lifestyle.

The first step toward more conscious consumption is reflection. Without a clear understanding of why and how you consume, any change remains superficial. Questions such as "Why am I buying this product?", "What feeling am I trying to compensate for?", or "Do I really need this?" are crucial to uncovering the true motives behind your behavior. A consumption diary can help here, in which you document every purchase and the motives behind it. Studies show that writing down purchasing decisions increases awareness and reduces impulsive behavior (Fujita et al., 2006). However, reflecting on your own consumer behavior goes beyond simple questions. It requires a deeper engagement with the emotional and social triggers that influence purchasing decisions. Often, it is unconscious patterns that drive consumption. For example, buying a new product may be an attempt to relieve stress, gain social recognition, or regain a sense of control over one's life. By analyzing your consumption habits, you can identify these patterns and begin to question them.

A consumption diary is a particularly effective tool to support this reflection. Not only should you note what you buy, but also how you feel before, during, and after the purchase. Supplement your entries with observations about whether the purchase was planned or impulsive, and which external stimuli—such as advertising or social media—influenced you. This method helps you to make more conscious decisions and to recognize patterns that previously went unnoticed.

An example can illustrate the effectiveness of this method: A young woman who regularly buys clothes realizes after several weeks of documentation that she shops impulsively mainly after stressful workdays or arguments with friends. Through the diary, she recognizes that her purchases are often an attempt to compensate for emotional emptiness or dissatisfaction. This insight is the first step toward developing alternative strategies for emotion regulation, such as exercise, meditation, or building social connections.

However, reflection alone is often not enough to change deeply rooted behavioral patterns. It should be complemented by targeted measures aimed at dealing more consciously with consumer stimuli. One possibility is to set concrete goals, such as limiting spontaneous purchases or introducing "waiting periods" before every major acquisition. Such strategies not only promote self-control but also help to develop a new relationship with consumption in the long term. In addition to individual reflection, exchanging ideas with others can be helpful. Discuss your experiences with friends or in online communities focused on sustainable consumption. Dialogue can not only open up new perspectives but also motivate you to work on your own behavior. Studies show that social support plays an important role in establishing new habits, as it provides positive reinforcement and reduces feelings of isolation (Bandura, 1986). In the long run, reflecting on your own consumer behavior is not only a means to reduce impulsive purchases but also a foundation for a more conscious and fulfilling life. By defining your values and needs more clearly, you can make decisions that sustainably satisfy not only your material but also your emotional and social needs.

An essential aspect of sustainable change is the establishment of new habits. Habits are deeply anchored in our brains and often influence our behavior without us being aware of it. They arise from repeated actions that become automated over time and play a crucial role in how we deal with our emotions and needs. Especially in the context of consumer addiction, these patterns are of central importance, as they often serve as automated responses to stress, boredom, or negative feelings.

For example, if you tend to shop online after a stressful workday, this is a learned behavior that your brain associates with a reward effect. To break this cycle, it is necessary to consciously create alternatives. Instead of regulating your emotions through consumption, you could turn to activities that produce similar positive effects but are more sustainable in the long term. Hobbies such as cooking, making music, or sports can help reduce stress while bringing joy and fulfillment. Mindfulness practices such as meditation or a walk in nature also offer an effective way to relax and clear your mind.

However, for new routines to actually replace old patterns, consistent practice is required. The brain needs time to create new neural connections and overwrite existing ones. Experts often speak of a minimum duration of 21 to 66 days to establish a new habit (Lally et al., 2010). During this phase, it is important to set realistic and achievable goals to avoid disappointment and setbacks. A small but conscious step, such as refraining from buying a particular product, can make a big difference, as it strengthens the sense of control and self-efficacy. Another supportive strategy is to visualize your goals and the positive effects that change will bring. For example, if you imagine how refraining from impulsive purchases leads to financial freedom or more time for personal interests, this further motivates you to stick to the new habit. Creating incentives—such as a reward for a successful week without unnecessary purchases—can also help maintain motivation.

Setbacks should not be seen as failure, but as part of the learning process. It is completely normal to occasionally fall back into old patterns. The important thing is not to be discouraged by these moments, but to see them as an opportunity to better understand your own triggers and to master future challenges more effectively. Long-term change is most successful when accompanied by a clear awareness of your own values. Ask yourself which things in your life are truly important and how your consumer behavior aligns with these values. This approach creates a stronger internal connection to the new habits and helps to integrate them as part of your identity. Instead of being someone who "buys less," you could see yourself as someone who lives consciously and sustainably. Transforming old habits into new, positive routines is a process that requires patience and perseverance. But every step along this path, no matter how small, brings you closer to a life less defined by consumption and more by conscious decisions.

A practical example illustrates this process: Paul, a 42-year-old engineer, decided to make his consumption more sustainable after noticing that he regularly bought unnecessary tech products. He began to plan his purchases consciously and to wait at least 24 hours before making a buying decision. This delay gave him time to reconsider his needs and led him to avoid many impulsive purchases. In addition, Paul kept a list of alternative activities he could try when he felt the urge to buy, such as sports or reading. This step-by-step approach helped him to break his old consumption patterns sustainably.

In addition to individual strategies, the social dimension is also of great importance. Changes are easier to implement when accompanied by a supportive environment. Share your goals with friends or family and look for like-minded people who share similar values. A supportive community can not only provide motivation but also reduce the social pressure that often leads to consumer behavior.

Practical Tip

Harness the power of rituals to consolidate new habits. A conscious morning ritual, in which you reflect on your goals for the day, for example, can help strengthen your mindfulness and self-control.

Sustainable change also requires a clear vision. Imagine what your life will look like once you have successfully changed your consumption habits. Visualization techniques can help anchor this vision in your consciousness and serve as a driving force for long-term change. At the same time, you should be aware that changes are necessary not only on an individual level but also on a societal one. Your contribution to more conscious consumer behavior can be part of a larger movement for sustainability and social justice.

Summary

- **Reflection as the foundation for change:**
  Sustainable change in consumer behavior begins with conscious reflection on your own purchasing habits and the underlying motives. Keeping a consumption diary and questioning impulses ("Do I really need this?") help to identify emotional triggers and unconscious patterns. These insights create a basis for making more conscious decisions and reducing impulsive behavior.
- **Establishing new routines and strategies:**
  Creating alternative behaviors, such as introducing "waiting periods" before purchases or focusing on hobbies and activities for emotion regulation, supports overcoming old consumption patterns. Realistic goals, visualization techniques, and reward systems strengthen motivation and promote long-term change. Setbacks are part of the process and should be seen as learning opportunities.
- **Social support and societal dimension:**
  A supportive environment of like-minded people and conscious social interactions make change easier and reduce the societal pressure that often leads to excessive consumption. Personal transformation not only contributes to a more fulfilling life but also makes an important contribution to sustainability and social responsibility.

Sustainable change requires reflection, realistic goals, and the establishment of new routines. Relapses are part of the process and offer the opportunity for further development. With mindfulness, a supportive environment, and clear goals, you can transform your consumption habits in the long term and have a positive impact on your life and your environment.

7.2 Dealing with Relapses: Learning from Mistakes

> **Example**
>
> In this section, you will learn how to cope with relapses on the path to more conscious consumer behavior and why they should not be seen as failure, but as learning opportunities.

Every change—whether a new attitude toward consumption or a long-term lifestyle adjustment—does not proceed linearly. Relapses are a natural part of the process and should be seen neither as failure nor as a reason to give up. Rather, they offer a valuable opportunity to recognize underlying patterns and develop new, more effective strategies. How you deal with relapses often determines whether a change will be lasting or not.

A relapse often occurs in moments of high emotional stress or in stressful situations, as old coping patterns are reactivated during such times. These patterns are often deeply embedded in the psychological structure and represent a seemingly easy way out to deal with negative feelings such as anxiety, frustration, or loneliness. In this context, the act of buying serves not only as a short-term distraction but also as an attempt to restore emotional balance. Studies show that especially impulsive purchases play a central role in such phases, as they are quickly accessible and promise immediate reward (Rook, 1987). The urge to reward oneself with luxury goods or new products can create the feeling of regaining control over one's life or gaining social recognition.

But this form of "self-medication" is problematic, as it only addresses symptoms and not the actual causes of emotional distress. The fleeting relief that comes from buying is often followed by a wave of negative emotions such as guilt or shame. These not only intensify the original problem but can further reinforce the relapse by further undermining the sense of control (Dittmar, 2008). The cycle of short-term reward and long-term burden thus leads to a dynamic that makes it difficult for those affected to break away from their old consumption patterns without targeted interventions and support measures.

In addition, stressful situations often impair the cognitive resources necessary for self-control and conscious decision-making. People in such phases tend to act more impulsively and prefer short-term solutions over long-term consequences. This "cognitive overload" means that rational considerations, such as the financial consequences of a relapse, recede into the background and the urge for immediate relief takes precedence (Baumeister & Heatherton, 1996). In such moments, the social and cultural pressure, reinforced by advertising and social media, can further contribute to the risk of relapse. The portrayal of luxury goods and consumer-oriented lifestyles as symbols of success and happiness reinforces the tendency to seek short-term satisfaction through purchases.

In the long term, repeated relapses can not only exacerbate financial problems but also impair the self-esteem of those affected. The feeling of failure after a relapse can lead those affected to question their ability to make changes. These negative emotions increase the likelihood of further relapses, as consumption is again used as a means of coping with these feelings. This creates a vicious cycle that is difficult to break without targeted interventions and support.

To interrupt this relapse cycle, it is crucial to identify the triggers and develop alternative strategies for emotion regulation. Mindfulness exercises, such as consciously perceiving emotions without acting immediately, can help interrupt the automatic urge to buy. Support from social networks or professional counseling is also of great importance in learning new coping strategies and preventing relapses. Relapses should also not be seen as complete failure, but as part of the change process, which requires time and practice.

Reflecting on the mechanisms that lead to a relapse is a crucial step toward establishing healthy and self-determined consumer behavior in the long term. By understanding their emotional and cognitive patterns, those affected can work specifically on their weaknesses and strive for sustainable change.

An example shows how a relapse can be analyzed and used: Martin, a 42-year-old teacher, decided to change his impulsive consumer behavior after repeatedly getting into financial difficulties. After several successful months of restraint, he experienced a stressful period at work. To calm himself, he spontaneously bought an expensive smartwatch that he actually could not afford. At first, he felt relief, but soon frustration set in. Instead of condemning himself, Martin reflected on the situation. He realized that the purchase was a reaction to his stress and developed alternative strategies, such as targeted relaxation exercises and regular breaks, to better cope with such moments in the future.

Relapses offer the opportunity to gain deeper insights into personal behavioral patterns. They reveal which triggers control the behavior and which emotional needs have not yet been adequately addressed. This can lead to more sustainable change by identifying specific weaknesses and addressing them directly. Another important aspect is self-care: Those who respond to relapses with self-criticism or shame risk falling back into old patterns. A compassionate approach to oneself, on the other hand, promotes resilience and the willingness to learn from mistakes (Neff, 2011).

Practical Tip

Keep a relapse diary. Note what happened, which emotions played a role, and which triggers could be identified. This helps to recognize patterns and develop preventive strategies.

In the long term, a mindful approach to relapses can help strengthen confidence in your ability to change. It is important to focus on progress rather than overemphasizing setbacks. Every step in the right direction counts, even if there are moments of pausing or reorientation in between.

The social environment also plays an important role in dealing with relapses. Support from friends, family, or professional companions can help change the perspective on setbacks and provide new impulses. Open communication about challenges and fears also fosters a sense of cohesion and acceptance.

Important

Relapses are not a defeat, but part of the process. Use them to refine your strategy and better understand your emotional needs.

This section shows that relapses are not a weakness, but a natural and valuable opportunity to learn from mistakes. They offer the chance to consciously continue the change process and make it more successful in the long term. A reflective approach to setbacks strengthens resilience and promotes sustainable consumer behavior.

Summary

- **Understanding relapses as learning opportunities**: Relapses are a natural part of any change process and should not be interpreted as failure. Instead, they offer the opportunity to analyze emotional triggers and behavioral patterns and to work on them specifically to enable sustainable change.

- **Identifying triggers and coping strategies**: Stress, negative emotions, or social influences are common triggers for relapses. Through conscious reflection and tools such as a relapse diary, individual patterns can be recognized and preventive strategies, such as mindfulness or social support, can be developed.
- **Promoting self-care and social support**: A compassionate approach to oneself and the inclusion of a supportive social environment are essential for coping with setbacks and making the change process successful in the long term. Every relapse can be used to strengthen resilience and self-confidence.

Relapses are part of the change process. This section has shown how you can learn from these experiences and develop new strategies to emerge stronger. Conscious reflection and a compassionate approach to yourself are the keys to consistently continuing on your own path.

7.3 Building a Self-Determined Life Beyond Consumer Addiction

Example

In this section, you will learn how to create a life based on your inner values rather than material consumption, and which steps can support you in developing an authentic and sustainable lifestyle.

Leaving consumer addiction behind means far more than controlling impulsive buying behavior or reducing material desires. It is a deeper process that requires redefining your approach to life and freeing yourself from external expectations. A self-determined life is based on values that are independent of possessions and social status, opening up the possibility of finding authentic relationships and personal fulfillment.

A crucial step in this process is clarifying your own values. Values are the cornerstones that guide our lives and influence our decisions. They serve as an inner compass and give our actions deeper meaning. Yet in a world flooded with consumer incentives, these values often fade into the background. Instead, many people orient themselves toward external standards shaped by advertising, social media, and cultural ideals. These external influences often convey the message that happiness and success are attainable through the possession of material goods. For example, many people strive for a "perfect" life symbolized by the ownership of luxury items. However, this pursuit rarely leads to lasting satisfaction, as it is driven by external influences and often ignores one's own needs (Kasser, 2002).

The problem lies in the fact that consumption is portrayed in our society as a means of self-actualization and identity formation. Advertising companies deliberately create associations between their products and certain values, such as freedom, individuality, or social status. Yet these values are often constructed and have little to do with an individual's actual needs or goals. People who align their lives with such external ideals often experience a discrepancy between what they truly want and what they are told they should want. This discrepancy can lead to dissatisfaction, frustration, and a sense of alienation (Dittmar, 2008).

Another aspect is the influence of social comparison. In an increasingly digital world, where social media like Instagram or TikTok dominate daily life, consumption is often put on public display. This intensifies the pressure to measure up to these ideals. People who frequently compare themselves to others are more likely to measure their satisfaction by their material possessions. But rather than boosting self-esteem, this focus on consumer goods often leads to feelings of inadequacy, as comparisons with others are rarely realistic and usually reflect an idealized version of reality.

Clarifying your own values therefore requires conscious reflection. It is about pausing and asking yourself: What is truly important to me? What goals am I pursuing? What things enrich my life in a deeper and more sustainable way? The answers to these questions can help establish a stronger connection to your own needs and break free from the expectations of others. People who have clearly defined their values can more easily recognize which purchasing decisions are truly in line with their beliefs and which are merely based on external pressure.

A practical approach to clarifying your own values is the so-called values list, in which individuals are asked to name their most important values and rank them by priority. This exercise helps to reflect on the significance of material and immaterial aspects in one's own life. For example, values such as family, health, or creativity may be placed far above material possessions. When these priorities are clear, it becomes easier to make decisions that are satisfying in the long term, rather than just fulfilling short-term needs.

> **Important**
>
> Clarifying your own values is not a one-time act, but an ongoing process. It is helpful to pause regularly and review your priorities, especially in a world that is constantly trying to draw our attention to external standards.

By becoming aware of their values and detaching from external influences, people can develop a more authentic and fulfilling relationship with consumption. They realize that the value of life does not lie in the quantity or price of acquired goods, but in the experiences, relationships, and beliefs that truly matter to them. This shift in perspective can not only enhance individual well-being but also contribute to a more sustainable and less consumption-oriented society.

Working toward a values-based life begins with conscious reflection. Questions such as "What is truly important to me?" or "Which experiences have brought me the deepest fulfillment?" help to break away from superficial consumer goals. Mindfulness techniques and journaling can be supportive tools in answering these questions. Research shows that people who consciously align their decisions with their values exhibit higher life satisfaction and resilience (Ryan & Deci, 2001).

A practical example shows how this transformation can succeed: Paul, a 42-year-old architect, describes how he went through a crisis after years of excessive consumption. "I had everything I had imagined—a big house, an expensive car—and yet I felt empty." Paul began to question his priorities and realized that time with his family and creative projects meant more to him than material possessions. Today, he lives minimally and consciously invests in experiences that bring him joy, such as traveling or volunteer work.

In addition to clarifying values, it is important to find alternative sources of fulfillment. Instead of seeking short-term happiness through the purchase of new products, hobbies, social relationships, or personal growth can bring deeper and more lasting satisfaction. Activities such as sports, art, or meditation not only promote well-being but also strengthen the connection to one's own values. Social bonds are particularly significant. Studies show that close relationships with family and friends are the strongest predictor of long-term satisfaction (Harvard Study of Adult Development, 2015).

> **Practical Tip**
>
> Create a list of activities that bring you joy and have nothing to do with consumption. Regularly schedule time for these activities to create new sources of fulfillment.

A self-determined life also requires the courage to break away from societal expectations. Giving up status symbols or material possessions is often perceived as radical, but it is a powerful step toward inner freedom. Minimalism and conscious consumption are not strategies of deprivation, but means to make room for what is essential. The philosophy of "less is more" allows you to focus on what truly matters—relationships, experiences, and personal development (Fromm, 1976).

This approach requires a conscious engagement with your own values and goals. In a world dominated by advertising and social media, we are constantly encouraged to own more, consume faster, and define ourselves through material goods. Yet this very dynamic can lead to overwhelm, obscuring what is truly important in life. The decision to let go of unnecessary baggage is therefore not just an external act, but a profound process of inner transformation.

Minimalism is not a rigid rule, but an individual journey. For some, it means decluttering their wardrobe and limiting themselves to a few high-quality pieces of clothing. For others, it may be the conscious decision to spend less time on social media or to slow down daily life. The common denominator, however, is always the pursuit of greater clarity and quality of life. When we let go of the idea that our worth is defined by what we own, we can create space to connect with our deepest needs and desires.

An important aspect of this philosophy is the shift from "having" to "being." Erich Fromm emphasized that a fulfilled life is not found in the possession of things, but in the ability to have authentic experiences, nurture deep relationships, and realize oneself (Fromm, 1976). This change in perspective makes it possible to shift the focus from material to immaterial values, such as love, creativity, and community. It is not about giving up everything, but about making the conscious decision to keep only what truly makes a positive contribution to our lives (Hoffmann, 2024).

> **Reference to Exercise 9**
>
> Section 7.3 offers you a practical exercise for clarifying values and setting priorities. Exercise 9 in section 9.3.9 "Reflecting on Values and Setting Priorities" supports you in creating a more conscious life shaped not by consumer dependence, but by authentic values.

However, this path is not always easy. The pressure to conform to social norms is strong. Giving up status symbols can be perceived as giving up social status. But this is precisely where the strength of minimalism lies: it challenges us to define our identity independently of external factors. This means letting go of the expectation that certain brands, objects, or lifestyles are necessary to gain acceptance or recognition. Instead, you gain the freedom to focus on authentic values that promote long-term satisfaction and happiness. The positive effects of conscious reduction extend far beyond the individual. A minimalist lifestyle also has ecological and social benefits. Abstaining from excessive consumption helps conserve resources, reduce waste, and promote the demand for sustainable alternatives. At the same time, it sends a powerful signal to society that happiness and fulfillment do not depend on the constant accumulation of goods. It is a call to pause, reflect, and build a more conscious relationship with our needs and our environment.

This process is not without challenges. Relapses into old patterns are normal and should be seen as opportunities for reflection and further development. The goal is not to lead a perfect life, but to regain control over your own decisions and create an authentic life.

> **In Summary**
>
> - **Realignment with Values and Needs:**
>   The key to a self-determined life lies in the conscious reflection of your own values and needs. This realignment helps to break free from socially imposed consumer ideals and to make decisions based on authentic beliefs and long-term well-being.
> - **Promoting Alternative Sources of Fulfillment:**
>   Instead of seeking short-term gratification through consumption, the focus should be on immaterial values such as relationships, personal development, and creative activities. These sustainable sources of fulfillment foster satisfaction and resilience.
> - **Courage to Break Away from Societal Expectations:**
>   A minimalist lifestyle requires the courage to break away from social norms and status symbols. This makes it possible to define your own worth

independently of material possessions and to focus on a life characterized by authenticity and inner freedom.

Building a self-determined life beyond consumer addiction requires a realignment with values that are independent of material possessions. Through conscious reflection, seeking alternative sources of fulfillment, and the courage to break away from societal expectations, you can lead a life based on authenticity and inner contentment.

References

Bandura, A. (1986). *Social foundations of thought and action: A social cognitive theory.* Englewood Cliffs: Prentice-Hall.

Baumeister, R. F., & Heatherton, T. F. (1996). Self-regulation failure: An overview. *Psychological Inquiry, 7*(1), 1–15.

Dittmar, H. (2008). *Consumer culture, identity and well-being: the search for the „good life" and the „body perfect".* Psychology Press.

Fromm, E. (1976) *Haben oder Sein: Die seelischen Grundlagen einer neuen Gesellschaft.* Dtv.

Fujita, K., Trope, Y., Liberman, N., & Levin-Sagi, M. (2006). Construal levels and self-control. *Journal of Personality and Social Psychology, 90*(3), 351–367.

Harvard Study of Adult Development (2015). *What Makes a Good Life?* Harvard Gazette.

Hoffmann, O. (2024). *Wozu?—Über den Wert der Dinge.* Metropolis.

Kasser, T. (2002). *The high price of materialism.* MIT Press.

Lally, P., Van Jaarsveld, C. H., Potts, H. W., & Wardle, J. (2010). How are habits formed: Modelling habit formation in the real world. *European Journal of Social Psychology, 40*(6), 998–1009.

Neff, K. (2011). *Self-Compassion: Stop Beating Yourself Up and Leave Insecurity Behind.* New York: William Morrow.

Rook, D. W. (1987). The buying impulse. *Journal of Consumer Research, 14*(2), 189–199.

Ryan, R. M., & Deci, E. L. (2001). On happiness and human potentials: A review of research on hedonic and eudaimonic well-being. *Annual Review of Psychology, 52*(1), 141–166.

Further Reading

Baumeister, R. F., & Tierney, J. (2012). *Willpower: Rediscovering the greatest human strength.* Penguin.

Baumeister, R. F., & Vohs, K. D. (2007). *Self-regulation and the executive function of the self.* Cambridge University Press.

Csikszentmihalyi, M. (1990). *Flow: The psychology of optimal experience.* Harper & Row.

Duhigg, C. (2012). *The power of habit: Why we do what we do in life and business.* New York: Random House.

Hirschman, E. C. (1992). The consciousness of addiction: Toward a general theory of compulsive consumption. *Journal of Consumer Research, 19*(2), 155–179.

Kross, E., & Ayduk, O. (2017). Self-distancing: theory, research, and current directions. *Advances in Experimental Social Psychology, 55*, 81–136.

Prochaska, J. O., & DiClemente, C. C. (1983). Stages and processes of self-change of smoking: Toward an integrative model of change. *Journal of Consulting and Clinical Psychology, 51*(3), 390–395.

Thaler, R. H., & Sunstein, C. R. (2008). *Nudge: Improving decisions about health, wealth, and happiness.* Yale University Press.

Verplanken, B., & Wood, W. (2006). Interventions to break and create consumer habits. *Journal of Public Policy & Marketing, 25*(1), 90–103.

Wood, W., & Neal, D. T. (2007). A new look at habits and the habit-goal interface. *Psychological Review, 114*(4), 843–863.

8

Conclusion: A Conscious Approach to Consumption

Abstract The concluding chapter reflects on the central findings of the book and offers a final perspective on conscious consumption. It discusses what it means to be free from consumption addiction and the challenges involved in regulating one's own consumption in the long term. In addition, it provides an outlook on how a reflective approach to consumption could contribute to a more sustainable economic order at the societal level.

The journey toward a more conscious life does not end with the realization of how consumption influences our behavior and society. It begins right here. Chapter 8 is both a conclusion and a new beginning—an invitation to integrate what you have learned into your daily life and to develop a new attitude toward consumption. It is not just about owning or buying less, but about recognizing the true value of things, experiences, and relationships. This chapter inspires you to continue the transformation in your life, to develop sustainable habits, and to free yourself from the constraints of consumerism. It shows ways in which you can find freedom and fulfillment beyond materialism.

O. Hoffmann, *Rethink Consumption*, https://doi.org/10.1007/978-3-662-72946-5_8

8.1   What Does it Mean to be Free From Consumer Addiction?

> **Example**
>
> In this section, you will learn how a conscious and healthy approach to consumption not only means freedom from addiction, but also enables well-being, satisfaction, and a new perspective on life.

Being free from consumer addiction means more than simply no longer making impulsive purchases. It is a state of inner independence in which material possessions no longer serve as a means of self-definition. This freedom is accompanied by a profound shift in the perception of values, relationships, and the meaning of one's own life. It marks the transition from a consumption-oriented identity to a lifestyle characterized by conscious being and authentic experiences. But what exactly characterizes this freedom, and how does it affect well-being?

People who have freed themselves from consumer addiction often report a sense of lightness and control over their lives. Instead of being guided by external impulses, they make decisions that align with their inner values. This autonomy is a central feature of freedom from consumer addiction. The loss of compulsive buying makes it possible to invest resources—be it time, money, or energy—into other areas of life that bring greater satisfaction in the long term. As Kasser (2002) shows, an orientation toward intrinsic values such as personal growth, relationships, and community leads to more sustainable well-being than a focus on material goals.

An example illustrates this transformation: Anna, a 40-year-old teacher, reflects on her development after years of consumer dependence. She used to regularly buy clothes and decorative items to reward herself after stressful workdays. But the joy from her purchases never lasted long, and she increasingly felt burdened by the financial consequences. Today, she describes how she has learned to satisfy her needs in other ways—through hobbies, time with friends, and mindfulness exercises. "I no longer need things to feel good," she says. "I've realized that I am enough in myself." Anna's story shows how liberation from consumer dependence brings about not only external but also internal changes.

A crucial aspect of this freedom is the conscious engagement with the meaning of one's own life. Being free from consumer addiction means no longer tying your identity to external possessions. It opens up the possibility of asking deeper questions: What truly makes me happy? Which relationships are important to me? How can I use my resources more meaningfully? These questions often lead to a reorientation that increases personal well-being while also reducing the ecological footprint. As Fromm (1976) emphasizes, true freedom lies not in "having" but in "being"—in the ability to engage in authentic experiences and relationships.

Another key benefit of freedom from consumer addiction is relief from social pressure. In a world shaped by material comparisons, consciously refraining from excessive consumption creates space for more authenticity and independence. People who have freed themselves from this pressure report deeper satisfaction and serenity. They no longer have to define themselves by their possessions or try to keep up with the lifestyles of others. This inner calm not only has a positive effect on mental health but also fosters stronger, more honest relationships.

Practical Tip

Liberating yourself from consumer addiction requires patience and self-reflection. Start by clearly defining your values and finding out what truly matters to you. Mindfulness and a conscious approach to your needs can help you break free from the compulsion to consume.

However, freedom from consumer addiction does not mean abstinence in the traditional sense. It is not about giving up consumption entirely, but about placing it in a conscious and sustainable context. This not only creates more satisfaction in everyday life but also a deeper connection to your own needs and values. By learning to detach from external expectations, we gain a new perspective on what truly matters.

Summary

- **Inner independence and value orientation:** Freedom from consumer addiction means no longer defining yourself by material possessions and instead making decisions in line with your own values. This independence creates space for personal autonomy and a focus on intrinsic goals such as personal development, relationships, and community, which foster sustainable well-being.
- **Conscious living and reorientation:** Breaking free from consumer addiction opens up the possibility to question the meaning of your life and to reset your priorities. Instead of short-term satisfaction through purchases,

long-term contentment and a deeper connection to authentic experiences and relationships come to the fore.
- **Relief from social pressure and greater authenticity:** Consciously turning away from material comparisons creates a sense of calm that positively affects mental health and social relationships. Freedom from consumer addiction does not mean deprivation, but a sustainable approach to resources and needs that enables a more conscious, fulfilling life.

This section has shown that freedom from consumer addiction goes far beyond simply giving up impulsive purchases. It opens up space for conscious decisions, authentic relationships, and sustainable well-being. This freedom is not the end, but the beginning of a more conscious life based on inner values and genuine satisfaction.

8.2　Reflection and Outlook: Reshaping Your Life

Example

In this section, you will learn how to turn your insights about your consumption behavior into sustainable change. It inspires you to think beyond your own approach to consumption and to create a more conscious, fulfilling life.

Change begins with reflection. The journey you have started in this book was not an easy one—you have questioned your consumption behavior, discovered personal patterns, and perhaps accepted uncomfortable truths about yourself. But this reflection is the first step toward changing not only your consumption habits but also the way you shape your life in a sustainable way. It is not simply about buying less, but about building a new relationship with possessions, needs, and priorities.

The foundation of such change is awareness. Many of us consume automatically, without really questioning the motives or consequences. A moment of reflection, as encouraged in this section, can help you break free from this automation. Ask yourself questions like: "Why am I buying this?" or "What needs am I trying to fulfill with this purchase?" Such considerations bring clarity and create space for more conscious decisions. A real-life example shows how powerful reflection can be: Peter, a 42-year-old manager, realized that he made many of his purchases to relieve stress. Instead of continuing to consume, he began to develop alternative coping strategies, such as practicing mindfulness and exercise. This change not only led to less spending but also to increased well-being.

However, change is a process that does not come without setbacks. Old patterns are deeply rooted, and it is normal for them to resurface in difficult times. It is important not to view relapses as failures, but as opportunities to learn and adjust your strategies. For example, if you notice that you are making impulsive purchases again, use this moment as an opportunity for reflection: "What triggered this?" and "What alternatives do I have?" By analyzing such situations, you strengthen your ability to act more consciously in the future.

Another key aspect is creating a new vision for your life. Those who want to free themselves from the constraints of consumerism need positive goals that go beyond the acquisition of goods. Ask yourself: "What truly makes my life rich?" and "Which values do I want to live by?" Answers to these questions can help you reorder your priorities. For many people, this means spending more time with family and friends, pursuing creative passions, or strengthening their connection to nature. Such a vision not only gives your life depth but also a clear direction that frees you from the superficiality of consumption.

Practical Tip

Take time regularly to reflect on your progress. Write in a journal about what you have achieved and which challenges you have overcome. This process helps you stay motivated on your path and become aware of your successes.

Reshaping your life also means focusing on what is essential. Minimalism is a philosophy that inspires many people to simplify their lives and focus on what truly matters. It is not just about giving up material things, but about consciously experiencing the moment and appreciating what is already present (Millburn & Nicodemus, 2014). This attitude can help you break free from the illusion that more possessions automatically lead to more happiness.

Important

Change takes time and patience. Give yourself permission to make mistakes and celebrate small successes. Every step toward a more conscious life is a success.

> **Reference to Exercise 10**
>
> Exercise 10 in Sect. 9.3.10 "Create Your Personal Life Vision" helps you develop a personal life vision and define concrete steps to make your life more conscious and fulfilling. Use this exercise to clarify your values and goals and to sustainably change your everyday life.

This section is intended not only to motivate but also to inspire you to actively shape your life. Consumerism has taught us that happiness lies in external things—but true fulfillment is found within ourselves and in the depth of our relationships with others. Use the insights from this book to find your own path and to break free from the patterns that have shaped you so far.

Summary

- **Reflection as the foundation for change:** This section emphasizes the importance of consciously engaging with your own consumption patterns and motives. It shows how targeted questions and personal insights can lead to a deeper understanding of the emotional and social backgrounds of consumption. This reflection forms the basis for sustainable behavioral change.
- **Strategies for a more conscious lifestyle:** The focus is on developing alternative coping mechanisms, such as mindfulness and the realignment of priorities, to reduce impulsive buying behavior. Setbacks are viewed as learning opportunities to build more stable self-control and emotional resilience in the long term.
- **Creating a new life vision:** The section inspires you to discover values and goals beyond materialism, such as through minimalism, stronger interpersonal relationships, or the pursuit of personal growth. It shows how a life focused on what is essential can foster deeper happiness and satisfaction.

This section encourages you to turn reflection on your own consumption behavior into concrete changes. It shows how a more conscious, fulfilling life beyond consumption and materialism is possible, and how you can bring about sustainable change through small, continuous steps.

References

Fromm, E. (1976): *Haben oder Sein: Die seelischen Grundlagen einer neuen Gesellschaft.* Dtv.

Kasser, T. (2002). *The high price of materialism.* Cambridge: MIT Press.

Millburn, J., & Nicodemus, R. (2014). *Everything that remains: a memoir by the minimalists.* Asymmetrical Press.

Seligman, M. E. P. (2002). *Authentic happiness: Using the new positive psychology to realize your potential for lasting fulfillment.* Free Press.

9

Helpful Resources and Further Support

Abstract A wide range of practical resources can be found here: checklists for self-diagnosis, reflection exercises, and concrete instructions for behavioral change. Practical exercises, such as keeping a consumption diary or targeted mindfulness exercises, help to integrate the theoretical content into everyday life. In addition, further reading and professional contact points for those affected are recommended.

Change requires knowledge and orientation. Chapter 9 offers you a collection of valuable resources to help you deepen your understanding of consumer and luxury addiction and find practical support on your path to a more mindful life. From well-founded literature and informative websites to counseling centers, here you will find everything you need to further educate yourself and take concrete steps toward improving your consumption habits. This chapter is an invitation to continue your journey and discover new perspectives.

9.1 Recommended Literature

> **Example**
>
> In this section, you will find a selection of well-founded literature and relevant online resources to help you deepen your knowledge of consumer and luxury addiction and find practical solutions.

© The Author(s), under exclusive license to Springer-Verlag GmbH, DE, part of Springer Nature 2026

O. Hoffmann, *Rethink Consumption*, https://doi.org/10.1007/978-3-662-72946-5_9

The topic of consumer addiction is complex and requires a broad understanding that goes beyond the contents of this book. For readers who wish to delve deeper into the subject, a well-curated selection of literature and online resources offers invaluable added value. The following recommendations include scientific studies, practice-oriented guides, and informative websites that provide up-to-date insights and support.

A fundamental read that addresses the psychological and cultural mechanisms behind consumer behavior is *Consumer Culture, Identity and Well-Being* by Helga Dittmar (2008). Dittmar demonstrates how consumption is closely linked to the search for identity and well-being, and why materialistic values often lead to dissatisfaction. This work offers an in-depth analysis of the social dynamics of consumption and helps to understand the cultural influences on individual behaviors.

Another recommended book is *Die benötigte Sucht* by Oliver Hoffmann (2025). Here, I explain the theory behind consumer addiction in much greater detail and discuss at length how to overcome the multifactorial dependencies involved.

For a broader perspective on materialism and its impact on quality of life, Tim Kasser's *The High Price of Materialism* (2002) provides a comprehensive insight. Kasser argues that materialistic values not only diminish personal well-being but also strain social relationships and exacerbate ecological problems. This book is especially recommended for readers who want to understand the societal dimension of consumption and its impact on the environment.

A practical approach is offered by David T. Courtwright in *The Age of Addiction: How Bad Habits Became Big Business* (2019). Courtwright examines how companies deliberately promote addictive consumption patterns and why it is so difficult to escape them. The connection between personal behavior and economic interests is impressively illustrated here and provides food for thought on how to deal more consciously with consumer incentives.

For those seeking a psychological understanding of buying behavior, the classic *The Buying Impulse* by Dennis Rook (1987) offers valuable insights. Rook analyzes the dynamics of impulse buying and explains why spontaneous decisions are often influenced by emotional and cognitive biases. In addition, Erich Fromm describes in *To Have or To Be* (1976) how an orientation toward possession alienates people from authentic experiences and what alternatives exist for leading a more fulfilling life.

Practical Tip

Use the recommended sources not only for information gathering but also as a basis for self-reflection. Pause while reading and consider how the insights described might apply to your own behavior or environment.

The combination of scientific literature and practice-oriented resources offers a broad spectrum of knowledge that can help you approach consumption more consciously and critically. While the literature provides in-depth analyses and long-term perspectives, online resources often offer up-to-date insights and practical tips that can be easily integrated into everyday life.

In Summary

This section has presented you with a well-founded selection of books and resources that can serve as a foundation for a better understanding of consumer and luxury addiction. Use these recommendations to broaden your perspective and take concrete steps toward changing your consumption habits.

9.2   Checklists

Sometimes (in fact, quite often) it is surprisingly challenging to clearly reflect on your own behavior and recognize whether your individual consumption habits may already be problematic. Here, checklists can be a valuable first aid. They offer you the opportunity to question yourself in a simple and structured way. Through targeted questions aimed at specific behavioral patterns, you can find out whether your consumption already shows signs of addiction. Checklists are a valuable tool for recognizing early warning signs and potentially preventing bigger problems.

The key to successfully using a checklist lies in your honesty and self-reflection. As you go through the questions, consciously take time to think about your personal experiences and feelings. Questions such as "Do I often buy things impulsively that I don't really need?" or "Do I use shopping as a way to cope with negative emotions?" should be answered with genuine sincerity. The goal is not to judge or condemn yourself, but to gain clarity. A checklist gives you the opportunity to put your consumption behavior to the test and recognize whether it has already developed addictive traits. At the same time, I always recommend answering checklists in writing; writing things down significantly enhances the effect of personal reflection. Writing is not just a passive act of recording thoughts and feelings, but an active process of shaping them. When we write, we shape our thoughts and bring them into a structure that opens up new perspectives. We enter into a dialogue with ourselves and can deliberately influence our inner world. Writing can be used as an active tool to consciously steer mental processes. The act of writing enables us to recognize and transform destructive thought patterns. We can restructure our thoughts, channel emotions in new directions, and consciously decide which memories we want to use as resources for our present actions.

Even when we admit to ourselves that we are overconsuming, it is often difficult to recognize the underlying causes. Many people use shopping as a form of distraction or emotional regulation without being truly aware of it. By going through a checklist, you can identify these emotional triggers and understand the underlying need. It enables you to analyze your behavior and recognize clear patterns—for example, whether you buy more often to relieve stress or to reward yourself.

This self-assessment serves as the first step toward more conscious control of your consumption behavior. If you discover signs of problematic buying behavior, this is a good reason to consider possible changes or even seek professional help. Checklists help you regain control over your consumption before it completely controls you.

Self-assessment checklists thus give you a clear overview of your behaviors and help you make more conscious decisions. They are a first, important step toward a healthier and more balanced relationship with consumption.

I have divided the checklists in this book according to the most important topics into eight areas (with a total of 35 questions):

1. Checklist for the General Identification of Consumer Addiction
2. Emotional Triggers: A Checklist for Self-Reflection
3. Checklist for Financial Strain
4. Social and Occupational Impacts
5. The Role of Self-Esteem: A Psychological Checklist
6. Role of Impulsivity and Impulse Control
7. Cognitive Distortions and Shopping Addiction
8. Coping Checklists: Interventions and Change Strategies

1. Checklist for the General Identification of Consumer Addiction
The first checklist aims to identify the general signs and symptoms of consumer addiction. These questions are based on my findings and research on compulsive buying disorder.

1. **Do you frequently buy things you don't actually need?**
   Compulsive buyers often experience the urge to acquire things they don't need, just for the act of buying itself. This can be an indication that buying is more of an emotional than a practical act.
2. **Do you have difficulty controlling your spending?**
   A central feature of consumer addiction is the loss of control over one's own buying behavior. Many affected individuals report that, despite negative consequences (e.g., debt), they are unable to change their behavior.
3. **Do you spend a lot of time thinking about or planning purchases?**
   People with consumer addiction often obsessively think about shopping, plan their next purchase, or focus on things they want to buy in the future. This behavior can be a sign that consumption has taken up an excessive place in their lives.
4. **Do you feel guilt or regret after making a purchase?**
   Many affected individuals report a brief high after a purchase, followed by feelings of guilt or shame because they know the purchase was unnecessary or worsened their financial situation.
5. **Have your purchases had negative effects on your finances or social relationships?**
   Consumer addiction can lead to significant financial problems and social conflicts, especially when the behavior is kept secret from family or friends.
6. **When was the last time you were truly happy?**
   This question can be a starting point for effectively classifying individual consumer addiction.

2. Emotional Triggers: A Checklist for Self-Reflection
Emotions play a central role in the development and maintenance of consumer addiction. Many affected individuals use shopping as a coping strategy to deal with negative feelings such as boredom, anxiety, or loneliness.

1. **Do you shop to cope with negative emotions (e.g., stress, sadness, loneliness)?**
   Compulsive buyers tend to use shopping as a means of emotional coping. This behavior is often referred to as "emotional buying" and may indicate deeper psychological issues.
2. **Do you often feel lonely or bored and turn to shopping to feel better?**
   Boredom and loneliness are common emotional triggers for consumer addiction. Affected individuals report using shopping to temporarily gain a sense of fulfillment or social interaction.
3. **Do you experience a "high" after shopping that quickly fades?**
   The release of dopamine during shopping leads to a brief feeling of happiness, which quickly subsides. Many with consumer addiction then feel a strong urge to restore this state by shopping again.
4. **Do you consciously avoid situations that remind you of your shopping addiction (e.g., malls or online shops)?**
   Some affected individuals recognize their addiction and try to avoid situations where they might buy impulsively. This avoidance behavior is often a sign that the problem runs deeper than mere "shopping habits."

3. Checklist for Financial Strain

A key feature of consumer addiction is the financial strain it causes. Many affected individuals fall into significant debt due to their uncontrolled shopping, which further increases psychological stress.

1. **Do you have trouble paying your bills on time because you spend too much money on unnecessary purchases?**
   Financial stress is often one of the first signs of problematic buying behavior. Many with consumer addiction use money intended for important expenses like rent or bills to make impulsive purchases.
2. **Do you use credit cards or loans to finance your purchases?**
   The use of credit or installment payments is a common feature among those with consumer addiction who can no longer cover their purchases from their regular income. This often leads to a debt spiral that is hard to escape.
3. **Do you hide purchases or give false information about your finances to your social circle to conceal your buying behavior?**
   Many affected individuals hide their purchases from family members or friends out of shame or fear of consequences. This secretive behavior is often a sign that the problem is out of control.

4. **Have you ever considered taking out a loan to pay off debts incurred from shopping?**
Taking out loans to cover debts from consumption is a dangerous warning sign and can lead to significant long-term financial instability.

4. Social and Occupational Impacts

The social and occupational impacts of consumer addiction can be just as severe as the financial consequences. Compulsive buying behavior often negatively affects relationships with friends, family, and colleagues, as those affected become increasingly isolated and trust within their environment erodes.

1. **Have you already lost relationships or friendships because your buying behavior was perceived as problematic?**
Consumer addiction often leads to tension in relationships, especially when those affected hide their shopping addiction from family members or partners. Secrecy, debt, and unspoken conflicts are common triggers for social isolation.
2. **Does your buying behavior affect your performance at work or school?**
Many affected individuals report that their thoughts constantly revolve around shopping, preventing them from focusing on their work or other important tasks. This lack of concentration and increasing financial strain can negatively impact job performance.
3. **Have you ever used work resources or materials for personal purchases?**
Some with consumer addiction turn to the workplace to support their shopping habit, whether by using company credit cards or secretly ordering goods during work hours. This can not only jeopardize employment but also have legal consequences.
4. **Do you withdraw from social activities to hide your buying behavior?**
Affected individuals often avoid social interactions, especially when they know their buying behavior is viewed critically. This isolation increases psychological stress and contributes to further deterioration of mental health.

5. The Role of Self-Esteem: A Psychological Checklist

Self-esteem issues are often a decisive factor in the development of consumer addiction. People with low self-esteem tend to use the purchase of consumer goods as a way to fill their inner emptiness or reward themselves.

1. **Do you feel better or more confident after shopping, even if the purchase was unnecessary?**
   People with consumer addiction often experience a short-term boost in self-esteem after a purchase, as they feel they have "treated" themselves. However, this effect is usually short-lived and quickly replaced by regret.
2. **Do you use shopping as a reward for personal achievements or to relieve stress?**
   Many affected individuals use shopping as a way to reward themselves, even though this has negative long-term consequences. This behavior reinforces the problem by creating a vicious cycle of consumption and guilt.
3. **Do you often compare yourself to others in terms of what you own?**
   Social comparisons play a key role in maintaining consumer addiction. In a society where consumer goods are seen as symbols of success and prosperity, many people feel pressured to keep up with others.
4. **Do you feel that your self-worth depends on the things you own?**
   People suffering from consumer addiction often attach disproportionate value to their possessions. This link between material goods and self-worth can further reinforce the behavior and impair the ability to break free from the addiction.

6. Role of Impulsivity and Impulse Control

Consumer addiction is often characterized by a lack of impulse control. Impulsive behaviors in the psychological context are often associated with affective states such as frustration, anxiety, or boredom. Consumers with impulse control disorders frequently resort to buying goods to feel better in the short term. This reinforces the addiction and can cause both psychological and financial problems in the long run.

1. **Do you often act impulsively when it comes to buying goods, without thinking about the consequences?**
   Impulsive buying behavior is a strong indicator of consumer addiction. It suggests that the need for immediate gratification outweighs consideration of long-term consequences.
2. **Do you feel unable to control your impulses when you see a product that interests you?**
   The inability to control buying impulses is another sign of problematic behavior and may indicate deeper psychological issues.

3. **Do you experience frustration or anger when you cannot make a purchase immediately?**
   This frustration effect is frequently observed in people with consumer addiction who can no longer control their buying behavior and feel strongly emotionally affected by restrictions or obstacles.
4. **Do you feel that shopping is a way to alleviate negative emotions?**
   Emotional purchases are often impulsive and serve to temporarily cope with negative feelings such as loneliness or frustration. This behavior often intensifies if it is not recognized and controlled.

7. Cognitive Distortions and Shopping Addiction

Cognitive distortions, such as rationalizing impulsive purchases or overemphasizing the importance of material goods, play an important role in maintaining consumer addiction. These thinking errors lead affected individuals to justify their spending or view purchases as necessary or deserved.

1. **Have you ever rationalized a purchase by telling yourself you "deserved" it, even though you know it's unnecessary?**
   Many affected individuals justify their purchases by presenting them as a reward or something necessary. These cognitive distortions reinforce the behavior and often prevent the real problem from being recognized.
2. **Do you believe that owning certain goods will improve your life?**
   The belief that material goods bring happiness or fulfillment is a widespread thought pattern among people with consumer addiction. This often leads to constant purchases without ever achieving the desired satisfaction.
3. **Do you often assume that "others" do it too, and therefore you should buy as well?**
   Social comparisons and the desire to keep up with others play a central role in the development of consumer addiction. This type of cognitive distortion often leads to impulsive and unnecessary purchases

8. Coping Checklists: Interventions and Change Strategies

In addition to self-identification, developing coping strategies is crucial for freeing oneself from consumer addiction. This checklist offers practical approaches to reflect on and change buying behavior.

1. **Question every purchase: Do I really need this?**
   A simple but effective strategy is to question every potential purchase. If the purchase is based on emotional impulses, it helps to take time and reconsider the purchase.
2. **Set financial limits and track your spending**
   Setting a clear budget and tracking expenses can help prevent impulsive purchases and regain control over your finances.
3. **Avoid credit cards or installment payments**
   Whenever possible, use cash or debit cards to keep better track of your spending. Avoid financing models that allow you to make purchases on credit, as these often lead to debt.
4. **Avoid "triggers" such as shopping malls or online shops when you are emotionally stressed**
   A conscious approach to shopping triggers can help prevent impulsive purchases. If you know you are prone to emotional shopping, you should actively avoid these situations.
5. **Actively seek alternative ways to cope with negative emotions?**
   Instead of shopping, affected individuals should develop alternative coping strategies, such as exercise, meditation, or talking with friends. These strategies help fill emotional gaps without resorting to consumer goods.
6. **Do you use professional help?**
   If you feel you have lost control over your buying behavior, do not hesitate to seek professional help. Psychotherapy, especially cognitive behavioral therapy, has proven to be an effective treatment for consumer addiction.
7. **Do you share your addiction experiences with others?**
   Self-help groups or online forums can provide valuable support. Sharing with others who have had similar experiences can help you feel less isolated and receive practical advice for coping with addiction.

Example

Self-assessment checklists offer a good first opportunity to recognize problematic buying behavior early and initiate the necessary steps for change. However, it is crucial that those affected not only recognize the symptoms of their behavior but also understand the underlying psychological mechanisms in order to bring about lasting change.

9.3 Practical Exercises

Engaging with consumption behavior and the underlying psychological mechanisms is an important step toward achieving long-term changes in everyday life. But insight alone is often not enough to break deeply rooted patterns. The practical exercises in this chapter serve as a bridge between theoretical understanding and concrete action. They are designed to help you reflect more consciously on your consumption behavior, recognize emotional triggers, and develop alternative strategies for meeting your needs.

These exercises are designed to address different needs and life situations. They offer both opportunities for self-reflection and approaches to actively try out new behaviors. The goal is to provide you with tools that will help you achieve not only short-term changes but also sustainable improvements in your approach to consumption and your personal values.

The exercises do not demand perfection, but rather encourage you to take small, mindful steps. Every moment of mindfulness, every considered decision, and every questioning of automated habits brings you closer to a more conscious and fulfilling life. Use these sections as an opportunity to actively take responsibility for your consumption behavior and shape the change you wish to see in yourself.

9.3.1 Exercise 1: Strengthening Mindfulness in Purchasing Behavior

This exercise aims to help you recognize the underlying mechanisms of your consumption habits and make more conscious decisions. It is based on the concept of mindfulness and helps you get to the root of the emotional triggers for impulsive buying behavior. Ideally, carry out the exercise in writing, either in a notebook or digitally, to document the results and reflect on them later.

Step 1: Emotional Self-Observation Before Buying
Before making a purchase—whether online or in a store—take a moment to pause. Ask yourself the following questions:

- **What am I feeling in this moment?** (e.g., boredom, stress, joy, uncertainty)
- **What thoughts are going through my mind?** (e.g., "I really need this," "This will make me happy," "This is a bargain")

- **What do I hope to gain from this purchase?** (e.g., reward, distraction, improvement of my life)

Write down your answers without judging them. The goal is to develop an awareness of the emotional and cognitive processes that trigger your urge to buy.

Step 2: Reflect on Your Buying Motivation
After identifying your emotions and thoughts, ask yourself:

- **Do I actually need this product, or am I responding to an emotional need?**
- **Will this purchase make a positive difference in my life in the long term, or is the joy only short-lived?**
- **Can I postpone the purchase and reconsider it later?**

If you identify the urge to buy as an emotional reaction, try to consciously delay it—even if only for a few hours. This delay creates space to view the decision more clearly.

Step 3: Develop Alternative Strategies
Instead of giving in to the impulse, develop alternative strategies to deal with the underlying emotions:

- **If you feel stressed:** Do a short breathing exercise or go outside for some fresh air.
- **If you feel lonely:** Reach out to a friend or family member to start a conversation.
- **If you feel bored:** Engage in a creative hobby, such as drawing, writing, or making music, or read a book.

These alternatives help you meet emotional needs in a healthier way, without falling into the cycle of addictive buying.

Step 4: Mindful Reflection After the Purchase
If you have made a purchase, consciously reflect on the experience:

- **How do I feel now, after making the purchase?**
- **Did the purchase meet my original expectation?**

- **What long-term effects might this purchase have on my finances, well-being, or lifestyle?**

Document your thoughts and emotions. The goal is to recognize patterns that will help you make more conscious decisions in the future.

Step 5: Create a "Needs List"

Instead of buying impulsively, keep a list of things you truly need or that could bring you long-term joy. Review this list regularly and weigh whether a particular purchase is still necessary or desirable. This list helps you avoid spontaneous impulse purchases and set priorities.

Long-Term Integration of the Exercise

Repeat this exercise over several weeks and observe how your purchasing behavior changes. Over time, you will notice that your awareness of your consumption patterns sharpens and you become better able to control emotionally driven buying impulses.

Conclusion

This exercise is not only intended to help you reflect on your consumption behavior, but also to develop a sustainable relationship with your needs and desires. You will learn to recognize emotional triggers and find alternative ways to deal with them. Ultimately, this not only strengthens your self-control, but also your sense of autonomy and satisfaction in everyday life.

9.3.2 Exercise 2: Analyzing Your Own Consumption Behavior

This exercise aims to raise your awareness of your personal consumption patterns, distinguish between compulsive buying and luxury addiction, and identify the emotional and social triggers behind your purchasing decisions. Set aside 20 to 30 minutes and follow the steps below.

Step 1: Create a Consumption Timeline

- List all purchases from the past two weeks. Indicate what you bought, how much it cost, and whether the purchase was planned or impulsive.
- Highlight those purchases that you found particularly significant or emotional (e.g., something you bought out of frustration, joy, or stress).

Step 2: Question Your Motives

- Select three purchases from your list that you would like to analyze in more detail. For each purchase, write:

  1. Why did you buy this product?
  2. What did you feel (e.g., before, during, and after the purchase)?
  3. Did you feel that the purchase fulfilled a need, or did it serve another purpose, such as coping with stress or seeking recognition?
  4. Did you have the impression before the purchase that this product would make you happier or more satisfied?

Step 3: Differentiate Between Compulsive Buying and Luxury Addiction

- Reflect on whether your buying behavior was more impulsive and focused on the act of buying itself (an indication of compulsive buying), or whether the purchase was strategic and aimed at the symbolic meaning of the product (an indication of luxury addiction).
- Note whether social media, advertising, or the desire for recognition influenced your decision.

Step 4: Assess the Impact

- Consider the emotional and financial consequences of your purchases. Did the purchase have positive long-term effects, or was the satisfaction only short-lived?
- Analyze whether you felt guilt, regret, or dissatisfaction after the purchase.

Step 5: Develop Alternative Strategies

- Consider how you could respond differently to similar triggers in the future (e.g., stress, social comparisons). Write down at least three concrete strategies for managing your emotions or social needs without making a purchase (e.g., going for a walk, talking with friends, engaging in creative activities).

Step 6: Self-Reflection and Goal Setting

- Finally, write a brief summary of your insights: What patterns have you discovered in your consumption behavior? How do you want to handle such situations more consciously in the future? Set a concrete goal to break the cycle of compulsive buying or luxury addiction.

Note Repeat this exercise regularly, e.g., every four weeks, to observe changes in your behavior and self-perception. Be sure to appreciate your progress, even if it seems small—every step toward more conscious consumption is a success.

9.3.3 Exercise 3: Reflection on Concrete Consumption Behavior

This exercise helps you recognize the emotional and social mechanisms behind your consumption behavior and deal with your needs more consciously. You can do this exercise regularly to promote long-term change.

Step 1: Review of the Past Week

- Make a list of all purchases you made in the past week. Note:
  - The item or service purchased.
  - The reason for the purchase (e.g., need, impulse, reward, stress management).
  - Your emotions before, during, and after the purchase (e.g., joy, nervousness, relief, guilt).

Step 2: Analyze the Triggers

- Review your list and identify emotional or social triggers for the purchases. Ask yourself:
  - Did I really need this purchase, or was I trying to fill an inner void?
  - Was my purchase inspired by external influences such as advertising or social media?
  - How long did the positive feeling after the purchase last?

Step 3: Clarify Needs

- List the needs that may have been behind the purchases (e.g., recognition, comfort, relaxation).
- Consider alternative ways to meet these needs. Examples:

- For recognition: Seek a conversation with friends or family.
- For comfort: Schedule time for self-care, such as a walk or meditation.
- For relaxation: Try a creative activity such as drawing or writing.

Step 4: Set Personal Goals

- Set a concrete goal for the coming week, e.g.:

  - "Before every purchase, I will pause for at least 10 minutes and ask myself if I really need this product."
  - "I will try alternative activities when I feel the urge to buy something impulsively."

Step 5: Reflection

- At the end of the week, reflect on how well you achieved your goals. What changes did you notice? Which strategies were particularly helpful?

9.3.4 Exercise 4: Reflection on Personal Consumption Triggers

Goal of the Exercise: This exercise helps you identify the personal triggers and emotional backgrounds of your consumption behavior. Through conscious reflection, you can recognize your triggers and develop strategies to prevent impulsive purchases.

Instructions

1. **Keep a consumption diary:** For one week, record all purchases you make—both large and small. Document the time, the item purchased, the price, and your emotional state before and after the purchase. Example questions you can ask yourself:

   - How did I feel before making the purchase? (e.g., stressed, bored, happy)
   - Why did I decide to buy the product? (e.g., saw a special offer, boredom, desire for reward)
   - How did I feel after the purchase? (e.g., relieved, proud, guilty)

2. **Analyze patterns:** At the end of the week, review your notes. Look for recurring triggers or emotions associated with your buying behavior. Ask yourself:

   - Are there certain situations in which I am particularly prone to making purchases?
   - Which feelings or thoughts most often drive me to buy?
   - Were the purchases necessary or more impulsive?

3. **Develop alternative strategies:** Based on your analysis, consider how you can respond differently in future situations. For example, if you find that you often shop out of boredom, you could plan a different activity instead (e.g., read a book, go for a walk, or engage in a creative activity).
4. **Reflect on successes and setbacks:** Continue the exercise for another month to document progress and challenges. At the end of each week, briefly write down what worked well and what you would like to improve.

9.3.5 Exercise 5: Consciously Questioning Purchase Impulses

Goal

This exercise helps you recognize, question, and make more conscious decisions about spontaneous purchase impulses. It supports you in seeing through the manipulative mechanisms of advertising and social media and reducing impulsive buying behavior.

Instructions
1. **Daily purchase reflection:**
   Take 10 minutes every evening to note all purchases of the day—whether online or offline. Briefly describe:

   - What did you buy?
   - Why did you buy it? (e.g., actual need, saw an ad, emotional mood)
   - How did you feel before, during, and after the purchase?

2. **Analyze purchase impulses:**
   The next time you feel a strong urge to buy something:

   - Pause briefly and take a deep breath.
   - Ask yourself the following questions:

Do I really need this product, or is it a spontaneous impulse?
How did I become aware of the product? (e.g., advertising, influencer, recommendation)
Will this product bring me long-term benefit or only short-term satisfaction?

– Record your thoughts in a journal or note-taking app.

3. **Introduce a waiting period:**
   For planned or impulsive purchases, set a personal waiting period:

   – For small purchases: At least 24 hours.
   – For larger purchases: At least one week. Use this time to reconsider your decision. Often, the urge to buy will subside during this period.

4. **Conscious consumption as a goal:**
   At the end of the week, consider:

   – How many purchases did you actually regret?
   – Which purchase decisions were thoughtful and necessary?
   – Which advertisements or content influenced you?

This exercise not only promotes self-reflection, but also helps you deal more consciously with advertising and social media and reduce impulsive buying behavior in the long term.

9.3.6 Exercise 6: The "Interrupting Impulses Strategy"

Goal: This exercise helps you recognize, consciously question, and control impulsive buying decisions before you act.

1. **Identifying the purchase impulse:** As soon as you feel the urge to buy something, pause and consciously notice the impulse. Ask yourself:

   – "What triggered this desire?" (e.g., advertising, social media, stress)
   – "How am I feeling right now?" (e.g., bored, stressed, lonely)

2. **The 24-hour rule:** Commit to waiting at least 24 hours before making the purchase. Use this time to consider the usefulness and necessity of the product.
3. **Find alternatives:** Consider how you can cope with the emotional trigger in another way. For example:

   – Go for a walk or exercise to relieve stress.

– Call a friend if you feel lonely.
– Engage in a creative activity such as drawing or writing.

4. **Consciously question the purchase:** After the waiting period, ask yourself the following questions:

   – "Do I really need this product, or did I just want to satisfy an emotional need?"
   – "Do I already have something similar at home?"
   – "How will I feel if I make this purchase—and how will I feel if I don't?"

5. **Reflection after the purchase:** If you decide to make the purchase, reflect on the process afterward:

   – "How did I feel while waiting?"
   – "Did the purchase meet my expectations?"

9.3.7 Exercise 7: Financial Reflection and Goal Setting

Goal: This exercise helps you thoroughly reflect on your financial situation, set clear priorities, and plan concrete steps to restore financial order. It consists of three consecutive phases that you should work through calmly and with sufficient time.

Phase 1: Taking Stock—Creating Transparency

1. **Gather all relevant documents:**
   Create an overview of your last three months of bank statements, credit card bills, and cash payments. Use digital tools if needed or print out the documents.
2. **Categorize your expenses:**
   Divide your expenses into three categories:

   – **Basic needs:** Rent, groceries, insurance
   – **Wants:** Leisure, shopping, subscriptions
   – **Unplanned expenses:** Impulse purchases, late fees. Add up the amounts in each category and determine their percentage of your total income.

3. Identify "invisible" expenses

Check for small, recurring items that you may not have consciously noticed before (e.g., coffee on the go, app purchases). These often add up to a significant amount.

Phase 2: Understanding Emotional Triggers

1. Keep a consumption diary:

For one week, record every purchase you make, including small amounts. For each entry, add:

- **Emotional state before the purchase** (e.g., stressed, bored)
- **Motivation for the purchase** (e.g., reward, distraction)

2. Reflect on the results

Analyze your consumption diary. Are there recurring emotional triggers for purchases? Do you notice patterns, such as shopping during stressful moments?

Phase 3: Set Goals and Plan Concrete Steps

1. Define financial goals:

Set three realistic, measurable goals, such as:

- "I will reduce my monthly spending on leisure activities by 20%."
- "I will build an emergency fund of €500 in six months."

2. Create a budget plan:

Use the 50/30/20 principle:

- 50% of your income for basic needs
- 30% for personal wants
- 20% for savings and debt repayment

3. Implement control mechanisms

- Set up automatic transfers for savings.
- Apply the 24-hour rule: For non-essential purchases, wait a day and then check if the purchase still seems necessary.
- Use financial apps to regularly monitor your progress.

9.3.8   Exercise 8: The Consumption and Values Diary

Goal of the exercise: This exercise helps you to consciously reflect on and shape the balance between "Having" and "Being" in your life. You will learn to analyze your purchasing decisions and their underlying motivations, and to shift your focus toward intangible values.

1. **Preparation:**

   - Get yourself a notebook or set up a digital note-taking app.
   - Divide each page into three columns with the headings: *What did I buy?*, *Why did I buy it?*, and *How do I feel afterwards?*.

2. **Implementation:**

   - For at least one week, record every product or service you purchase.
   - For each entry, reflect on why you made the purchase. Was it a necessary purchase? Was it for emotional satisfaction or social recognition?
   - Document afterwards how you feel after the purchase. Are you satisfied? Do you feel guilty, empty, or joyful?

3. **Reflection:**

   - At the end of the week, analyze your notes. Look for patterns: Do you buy more often for emotional or practical reasons? Which purchases actually increased your well-being?
   - Identify areas where you can make your consumption habits more conscious, and consider how you could focus more on "Being," for example through activities not related to consumption (e.g., time with family, nature, creative pursuits).

4. **Long-term integration:**

   - Set weekly or monthly goals to improve the balance between "Having" and "Being." For example, you might decide to consciously postpone a particular purchase impulse or replace it with a non-material activity.

9.3.9 Exercise 9: Reflecting on Values and Setting Priorities

Goal of the exercise: This exercise helps you identify and prioritize your personal values. It provides a foundation for building a life beyond consumer addiction, based on authenticity and inner satisfaction.

Instructions
1. **Preparation:**
   Set aside 20–30 minutes and find a quiet place where you will not be disturbed. Have paper and pen or a journal ready.
2. **Create a list of values:**
   Spontaneously write down all the values that seem important to you. Examples might include: family, health, freedom, creativity, security, friendship, growth, or sustainability.
3. **Prioritize:**
   From your list, select the five most important values. Rank them in order of significance to your life, starting with the value that means the most to you.
4. **Reflection:**
   For each of the five values, consider:

   - Why is this value important to me?
   - How is this value currently reflected in my life?
   - Are there areas where I neglect this value or should prioritize it differently?

5. **Action plan:**
   For each of the five values, write down a concrete action that could help anchor this value more firmly in your everyday life. For example: If "health" is a central value, you might decide to exercise regularly or eat more mindfully.
6. **Continuous review:**
   Set a goal to review and update your list of values regularly (e.g., monthly) to ensure that your priorities align with your life circumstances and goals.

9.3.10 Exercise 10: Create Your Personal Life Vision

Goal

This exercise helps you clarify your values and priorities and develop a clear vision for a conscious, fulfilling life beyond consumption and materialism.

Instructions

1. **Review and reflection:**

   - Take a sheet of paper or your journal and answer the following questions:

     What has truly made me happy in the past? Was it material things or experiences, relationships, achievements?
     Which purchases do I regret in hindsight? Why?
     When have I felt most in tune with myself and my values?

2. **Identify values:**

   - Write down three to five values that are especially important to you (e.g., family, health, creativity, social responsibility).
   - Consider how these values are currently reflected in your life and whether your consumption behavior is in harmony with them.

3. **Set goals:**

   - Formulate concrete goals that promote your values. For example:

     "I want to spend more time with my family instead of focusing on material possessions."
     "I want to consume more mindfully by considering before each purchase whether it is truly necessary."

4. **Plan steps:**

   - Develop practical steps to achieve your goals. These could include:

     Reducing impulse purchases by instituting a 24-hour waiting period before each purchase.
     Investing in experiences instead of things, e.g., a trip or a shared meal with friends.

5. **Visualization:**

   - Close your eyes and imagine what your life will look like when you implement these changes. How do you feel? What has improved?

6. **Regular review:**

  – Schedule a brief weekly reflection: Which steps have you implemented? Where are there still challenges? How can you continue?

Duration

30–45 minutes for the initial development, 10 minutes per week for review.

Afterword

For me, this book was not just a writing project, but a journey—a journey that led me to view our relationship with consumption, ownership, and the underlying psychological mechanisms from a completely new perspective. In a world dominated by advertising, social media, and material values, it is easy to lose sight of what matters. Yet, as I wrote, it became increasingly clear to me how deeply these issues permeate our lives and how profoundly they influence our thinking, feeling, and behavior.

I have learned that consumption is much more than the act of buying. It is a reflection of what drives us, what we lack, and what we seek. Often, we do not buy things, but rather the idea of happiness, fulfillment, or belonging. Yet this path rarely leads us to what we truly need. Instead, it distracts us from what really counts in life: genuine connections, meaningful experiences, and awareness of the present moment. With this book, I wanted not only to shed light on the mechanisms of consumerism and luxury addiction, but also to encourage you to pause and ask yourself the fundamental question: *What truly makes me happy?* The answers to this are different for each of us, but I hope that the reflections and exercises in this book will help you find your own answers.

Change is a process that requires time, patience, and courage. There are no quick fixes, and setbacks are part of the journey. Yet every small step toward a more conscious life is a step worth taking. If this book has helped broaden your perspective, encouraged you to reconsider your relationship with consumption, or inspired you to try something new, then it has fulfilled its purpose.

O. Hoffmann, *Rethink Consumption*, https://doi.org/10.1007/978-3-662-72946-5

In closing, I would like to thank you—for your openness, your time, and your commitment to engaging with such a central and at the same time challenging topic. The fact that you have read this book to the end shows that you are ready to make a change, and that is the most important step of all.

From the bottom of my heart, I wish you that you find your own path to a more mindful, more fulfilling life—a life not defined by consumption, but by the values and relationships that truly enrich you.